D0382095

For they sleep not,
except they have done mischief;
and their sleep is taken away,
unless they cause some to fall.

In all those many golden, honey days, before the Fall, I, Lucifer, enjoyed the full pleasures of heavenly paradise. Lovely. Sublime. Grand. Glorious. More than you can imagine.

So what did I, Lucifer, do to earn such anger and enmity from Him? What was so unforgivable that the only appropriate punishment was to have me tossed to the lava, to the flames, to the ice beyond the River Styx?

I WANTED TO BE AN AUTHOR.

You have discovered my scrapbook.
Do you turn away, or do you turn the page?

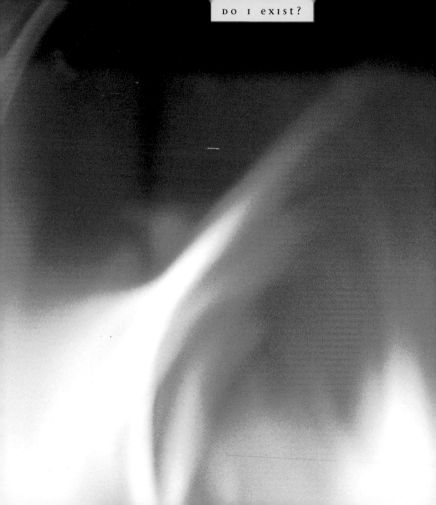

DO I EXIST?

is everything I say a Lie?

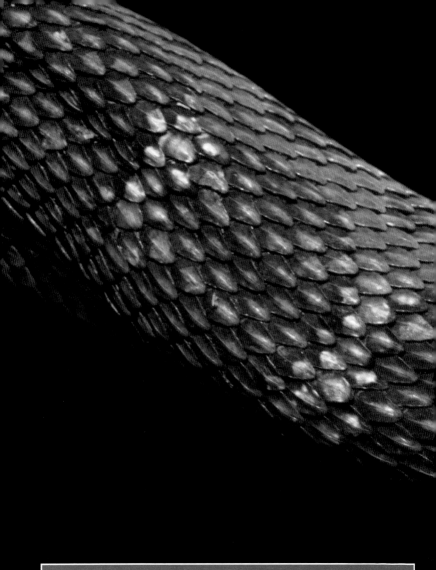

are what I do and what people claim I do the same?

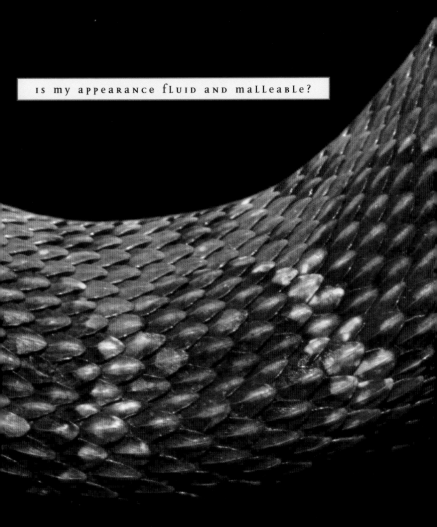

is my appearance fluid and malleable?

WOULD YOU CHANGE YOUR BEHAVIOR IF YOU KNEW WHAT I KNOW

DO I KNOW MORE THAN YOU?

can I be helpful?

to you?

tHe DevIL's mIscHIef

IN WHICH HIS OWN StORY IS tOLD
IN WORDS aND pICtUReS

An apology for the Devil—it must be remembered
that we have only heard one side of the case.
God has written all the books.

SAMUEL BUTLER

Ed Marquand

ABBevILLe pRess puBLIsHeRs
New YoRk ▸ LonDon ▸ paRIs

satan's LetteR

by MARK TWAIN

This is a strange place, an extraordinary place, and interesting. There is nothing resembling it at home. The people are all insane, the other animals are all insane, the earth is insane, Nature itself is insane. Man is a marvelous curiosity. When he is at his very very best he is a sort of low grade nickel-plated angel; at his worst he is unspeakable, unimaginable; and first and last and all the time he is a sarcasm. Yet he blandly and in all sincerity calls himself the "noblest work of God." This is the truth I am telling you. And this is not a new idea with him, he has talked it through all the ages, and believed it. Believed it, and found nobody among all his race to laugh at it.

Moreover—if I may put another strain upon you—he thinks he is the Creator's pet. He believes the Creator is proud of him; he even believes the Creator loves him; has a passion for him; sits up nights to admire him; yes, and watch over him and keep him out of trouble. He prays to Him, and thinks He listens. Isn't it a quaint idea? Fills his prayers with crude and bald and florid flatteries of Him, and thinks He sits and purrs over these extravagancies and enjoys them. He prays for help, and favor, and protection, every day; and does it with hopefulness and confidence, too, although no prayer of his has ever been answered. The daily affront, the daily defeat, do not discourage him, he goes on praying just the same. There is something almost fine about this perseverance. I must put one more strain upon you: he thinks he is going to heaven!

He has salaried teachers who tell him that. They also tell him there is a hell, of everlasting fire, and that he will go to it if he doesn't keep the Commandments. What are the Commandments? They are a curiosity. I will tell you about them by and by.

I call'd the devil, and he came,
And with awe his form I scan'd;
He is not ugly, and is not lame,
But really a handsome and charming man.
A man in the prime of life is the devil,
Obliging, a man of the world, and civil;
A diplomatist too, well skill'd in debate,
He talks quite glibly of church and state.

HEINRICH HEINE

make NO mistake

I dare you to find a single character in history or in literature or in art more fascinating than I. You won't, I assure you. Trust me on this. Who but I could have captivated so many dull minds and brilliant imaginations? We could list some contenders—a colorful crowd to be sure—but in the end a futile exercise, so let's get to the point. Me.

I admit that I am a patched-together piece of work; biology is not the force that governs my evolution. My persona has been in ferment for two thousand years. Was it created by me alone? By God Himself? By those who take my name in vain in the pursuit of power? By all of you in your own selfish ways? Just whose nimble fingers and clever hands have sculpted my visage?

Although those who claim to know me well deny authorship, theologians and peasants, scholars and politicians, the rich and the humble, the subtle and the bombastic, the cruel and the well-intentioned, the avant-garde and the archaic have each in turn added their strokes, bold and fine. I am malleable, it's true. But really, I am nobody but your fabrication.

тне ꝺevıL can вe an actoꝛ

He can be whatever he chooses. He is everywhere, the demon-
ologist Denis de Rougemont says. According to him, the evil
one wants to pretend that he does not exist. "I am nobody," he
says. But he is legion. By definition, he is an imperialist; he is a
gangster on the lookout for a kidnapping; he makes us doubt
the reality of the divine law; he is a liar, a tempter, a sophist,
and, though being nobody, he can impersonate as many beings
as there are in this world. This is true indeed, for the devil is
ever-changing in man's mind, unlike God, whose established
image, that of a good and wise old man, has remained constant
throughout the centuries. The devil likes to be modern.

KURT SELIGMANN

I am vastly more than some scaly imp

Although all cultures have their demons, my roots are Middle Eastern. Zarathustra, the Persian prophet from the seventh century B.C., built a religion that preceded Christianity. Zoroastrianism is based on belief in opposing forces of good and evil. The forces of light are led by Ahura Mazdah. The forces of dark, by Ahriman. Christianity owes much to the stories, characters, and lore of the Zoroasters. Study them and you will see curious similarities.

As Christianity spread, so did the growing need for me. As a counterforce to a personality as awe-inspiring as Jesus Christ, I helped the Church consolidate power by keeping the doubters, the straying souls, the troublesome thinkers, in line. High irony, to be sure, but as His reputation blossomed, so did mine.

Does it all come down to liturgical politics? Perhaps. I do not deny a keen interest in swaying the masses. Am I the ultimate political animal? Well, I can think of a fellow, a certain "savior," who enjoys this game at least as much as I do.

PAN AND DIONYSUS:
THE FAMILY RESEMBLANCE

I've been called Old Horny, an appellation I won't deny. Satyrs, my popular Greek cousins, were infamously naughty and randy. Pan and Dionysus were kings of the satyrs, and pagan cultures directed much worshipful energy their way.

As its influence spread, the voracious Church discovered how easily it could convert and conquer through cultural assimilation. Observing pagan devotion to local gods and goddesses, it cleverly appropriated their attributes and achievements for the sanctified members of its own saintly canon. Such spiritual makeovers were cheaper by far than any messy holy war, and so much more effective!

But Pan, Dionysus, and I were a breed apart. Our kind was too prickly for even the Christians to swallow. Since the Church could not absorb us into its pantheon of saints, it recast us as one irredeemably wicked soul. And so I, the Evildoer, emerged as half-man and half-goat, with horns, pointed ears, cloven hooves, a wicked smile, a glint in his eye. The Church knew that image was everything—and so did I.

HUBRIS PRECIPITATES THE FALL

Heaven is everything you can imagine, and much, much more. My life there was good, but even in Heaven, pride has its price.

I was the original fair-haired son, and my status as the best and the brightest didn't endear me to the other archangels. Even so, we all got along well enough—or so I thought. I admit to myself—in rare weak moments —that my pride did swell, perhaps overly. I probably should have seen trouble coming, but hubris is as blinding as the brightest sun.

As my daring and ambition grew by increments, I wanted more say, more power, more influence, over the affairs of Heaven. Jealousies and intrigues abounded. (For, yes, even in Heaven petty disputes rule the day.) I gathered allies and staked our position. A showdown was inevitable. But God, grown weary of our disputes, ordered our expulsion. Defeated, we fell. Clothed in the dust of my earthly exile, I looked back at the distant gates of Heaven, forever closed to me now. I knew it was over.

That part of my existence, anyway.

SANCTIMONIOUS
SAINT MICHAEL

Even before He flung me from Heaven, He and I had
our differences. If you believe the New Testament,
which presumes my eventual defeat, we will have the
ultimate fight on Judgment Day. We shall see.

faLLING DIfferentLy
every time

Writers clever and dim have described my fall from Grace. John Milton and Anatole France did it most splendidly. Milton's portrayal of me is flatteringly heroic, and France added a sensuous golden patina and a stunning ironic twist to his account. The Devil is nothing if not romantic, even about his own fall.

Me miserable! which way shall I flie
Infinite wrauth, and infinite despaire?
Which way I flie is Hell; my self am Hell;
And in the lowest deep a lower deep
Still threatning to devour me opens wide,
To which the Hell I suffer seems a Heav'n.

JOHN MILTON

Is this the Region, this the Soil, the Clime,
Said then the lost Arch-Angel, this the seat
That we must change for Heav'n, this mournful gloom
For that celestial light? Be it so, since he
Who now is Sovran can dispose and bid
What shall be right: fardest from him is best
Whom reason hath equald, force hath made supream
Above his equals. Farewel happy Fields
Where Joy for ever dwells: Hail horrours, hail
Infernal world, and thou profoundest Hell
Receive thy new Possessor: One who brings
A mind not to be chang'd by Place or Time.
The mind is its own place, and in it self
Can make a Heav'n of Hell, a Hell of Heav'n.
What matter where, if I be still the same,
And what I should be, all but less then he
Whom Thunder hath made greater? Here at least
We shall be free; th' Almighty hath not built
Here for his envy, will not drive us hence:
Here we may reign secure, and in my choyce
To reign is worth ambition though in Hell:
Better to reign in Hell, then serve in Heav'n.

JOHN MILTON
from *Paradise Lost*

I am Nectaire, like Lucifer, a fallen angel. Here, I recount the circumstances of Lucifer's fall from Heaven and his reemergence as Satan, who, along with his coterie of fallen angels (myself among them), would hold sway over mankind.

I knew him. He was the most beautiful of all the Seraphim. He shone with intelligence and daring. His great heart was big with all the virtues born of pride: frankness, courage, constancy in trial, indomitable hope. Long, long ago, ere Time was, in the boreal sky where gleam the seven magnetic stars, he dwelt in a palace of diamond and gold, where the air was ever tremulous with the beating of wings and with songs of triumph. *God, however, was jealous of Lucifer, and the angels* showed themselves, for the most part, incapable of lofty thoughts. . . . Lucifer, who held vile things in proud disdain, despised this rabble of commonplace spirits for ever wallowing in a life of feasts and pleasure. But to those who were possessed of a daring spirit, a restless soul, to those fired with a wild love of liberty, he proffered friendship, which was returned with adoration. These latter deserted in a mass the mountain of God and yielded to the Seraph the homage which That Other would fain have kept for himself alone. *Feelings of* liberty, curiosity, doubt . . . drew me towards the Seraph. I admired him, I loved him. I dwelt in his light.

After Lucifer and we his followers lost the war for heaven, we were flung to earth, where, in the dust, I remember, the Seraph remained awhile in meditation, his head buried in his hands. At length he raised his darkened visage. Now he was Satan, greater than Lucifer. Steadfast and loyal, we angels thronged about him. *Satan exhorted us to apply ourselves to the search for knowledge:* "In these silent realms where we are fallen, let us meditate, seeking the hidden causes of things; let us observe the course of Nature. . . . It is through pain that, suffering a first experience of Nature, we have been roused to know her and to subdue her. When she obeys us we shall be as gods. But even though she hide her mysteries for ever from us, deny us arms and keep the secret of the thunder, we still must needs congratulate ourselves on having known pain, for pain has revealed to us new feelings, more precious and more sweet than those experienced in eternal bliss, and inspired us with love and pity unknown to Heaven."

Satan and his angels became the teachers and advisers of mankind. To ancient peoples Satan showed in his various manifestations all the strength and beauty which it is given to mortals to conceive. His eyes had the sweetness of the wood-violet, his lips were brilliant with the ruby-red of the pomegranate, a down finer than the velvet of the peach covered his cheeks and his chin: his fair hair, wound like a diadem and knotted loosely on the crown of his head, was encircled with ivy. He charmed the wild beasts, and penetrating into the deep forests drew to him all wild spirits, every thing that climbed in trees and peered through the branches with wild and timid gaze. On all these creatures fierce and fearful, that lived on bitter berries and beneath whose hairy breasts a wild heart beat, half-human creatures of the woods—on all he bestowed loving-kindness and grace, and they followed him drunk with joy and beauty.

ANATOLE FRANCE
from *The Revolt of the Angels*

no place like hell

After the Fall I needed a home, a base, a little corner to call my own. In the *Aeneid*, written less than a century before Christ, the Roman poet Virgil created a grand Hades full of countless horrors. Picturesque beyond belief, it had ample room for an ever-increasing population of dead sinners. For centuries, theologians and preachers took straying souls and potential converts on imaginary journeys to Hades. By describing in detail every nightmarish discomfort a sinner could expect, they portrayed Hades as a most undesirable ultimate destination. It was the perfect threat to hold over weak and

Hell is paved with the skulls of priests.

ST. JOHN CHRYSOSTOM

That the saints may enjoy their beatitude and the
grace of God more abundantly, they are permitted to
see the punishment of the damned in Hell.

THOMAS AQUINAS

impressionable minds. So powerful was Virgil's vision
that all subsequent hells have been elaborations on his
basic floor plan.

Thirteen hundred years later, in the *Inferno*, Dante
visited Hades with Virgil as his guide. While posing
as a tourist, Dante managed to refurbish Hell with
the brilliance of an inspired architect. Never sparing a
wicked flourish, a gruesome vista, or a frightening folly,
his Hell was a triumph.

Milton's was no burned-out cinder cone either, but
his was a British effort. Stagey and boastful, impressive
in a Babylonian sense, it was not as generous in spirit as
other models. He added a convention hall and called it
Pandemonium, which implied chaos. But meetings there
were models of order. After all, I presided over them.

In the deepest pits of 'Ell,
Where the worst defaulters dwell
(Charcoal devils used as fuel as you require 'em),
There's some lovely coloured rays,
Pyrotechnical displays,
But you can't expect the burning to admire 'em!

EDGAR WALLACE

tundale

Now out of literary fashion, the story of Tundale is a
twelfth-century Irish version of a tour of Hell that
bears many of the same features as Virgil's *Aeneid* and
Dante's *Inferno*, with a few twists and wrinkles. The
pool you see here was a splendid addition, but notice

HeLL MoutHs

The mouth is interesting because
it's one of those places
where the dry outside moves
toward the slippery inside.

JENNY HOLZER

If God can have the "Pearly Gates" for His Heaven, I too can have a grand entranceway. I call my door "Hell Mouth," and some artists have put their best efforts into showing sinners entering Hell or devils and demons leaving Hell through this portal.

Stage designers for morality plays in the Middle Ages frequently built sets with Hell Mouths as entrances for characters. A little smoke, some flames, lots of noise, and you have a real crowd pleaser. Another sly trick of theirs was to costume the Devil to resemble a local merchant, cleric, or pompous member of the nobility. Both devices were guaranteed to enliven a dreary old play about virtue and higher purpose.

Hell hounds, all that be here,
Make you boun with boast and bere,
For to this fellowship in fere
There hies a ferly freke.
A noble morsel you have mun:
Jesu, that is God's Son,
Comes hither with us to won;
On him now ye you wreak!

ANONYMOUS
from *Everyman*

settled at last

A huge home with room
for my growing community.
Portals for grand entrances
and occasional exits.

It's time to go to work!

aDam anD eve in the garDen of eDen

It's such a familiar story, a cliché, really. There they were, this happy little couple living in bovine bliss in their splendid garden. I see the opportunity, approach her first, offer the apple. She tries a bite. She offers it to Adam. He takes a bite.

And the serpent said unto the woman,
Ye shall not surely die:
For God doth know that in the day ye eat thereof,
then your eyes shall be opened,
and ye shall be as gods,
knowing good and evil.

GENESIS 3:4–5

A sadder but wiser pair were they.

I have one lingering doubt, which puzzles me to this day.
It causes me to brood. I must have missed some essential
detail, some angle, some bit of wisdom that could explain
to me once and for all:

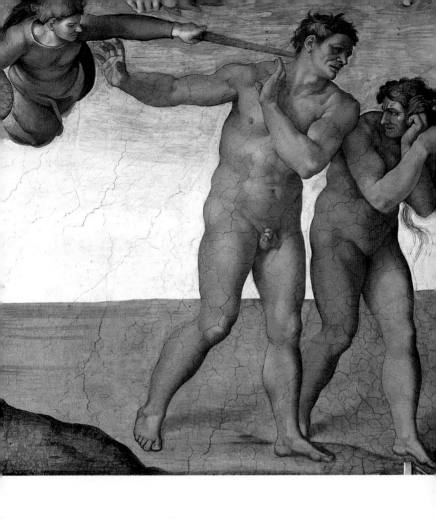

how could it have been so easy?

The Fallen Angel

aн, eve!

I wonder sometimes who tempted whom? That's the
way with temptation. Isn't it?

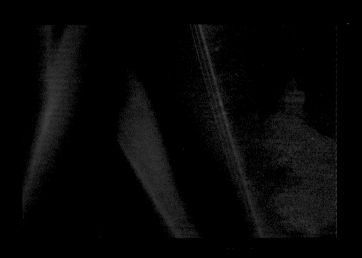

tHe LaDDeR of jUDGmeNt

How difficult it can be to reach Heaven, and how easy
it is to be snatched by demons and yanked to Hell.

I am no theologian, but this causes me more puzzle-
ment. If God likes humans so much, why does he want
so few of them to get into Heaven?

artists plumb the depths of their imaginations to describe hell

Unlike painters of landscapes or portraits, artists who depict Hell have had no real-life experience to guide them, so their work has either embellished their predecessors' notions or sprung fresh from their own fervid imaginations. Equally uninformed, their patrons didn't know what Hell looked like either, so how could they challenge the artists' visions? The imaginative leading the ignorant—a perfect partnership.

Usually commissioned by the Church to terrify wayward souls, painters decorated with wanton extravagance and abandon. Although I had no hand in directing them to depict the tortures they reveal, I find such scenes utterly fascinating.

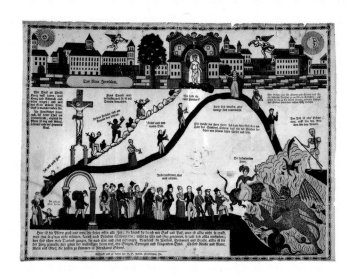

Heaven for climate, Hell for company.
J. M. BARRIE

as Heaven becomes an exclusive club, Hell becomes a popular destination

This road map to Heaven and Hell makes the path to salvation or damnation look as simple as a board game or miniature golf. And it can be, if you avoid those pesky sins and temptations!

Wir hielten jene für Thoren und Narren und für
ein höhnisch Beispiel, ja gar für ein Gelächter; jetzt
gehen sie ein zu des Herrn Freude, und wir Thoren
und Narren haben den rechten Weg verfehlt.

berufen, aber
d auserwählt.

Der Tod ist ohn' Erbar-
men, rafft hin den Rei-
chen, wie den Armen.

r: Ich habe kein Gefallen am
ern, daß sich der Sünder be-
ösen Wesen und lebe.

Die babylonische
Hure.

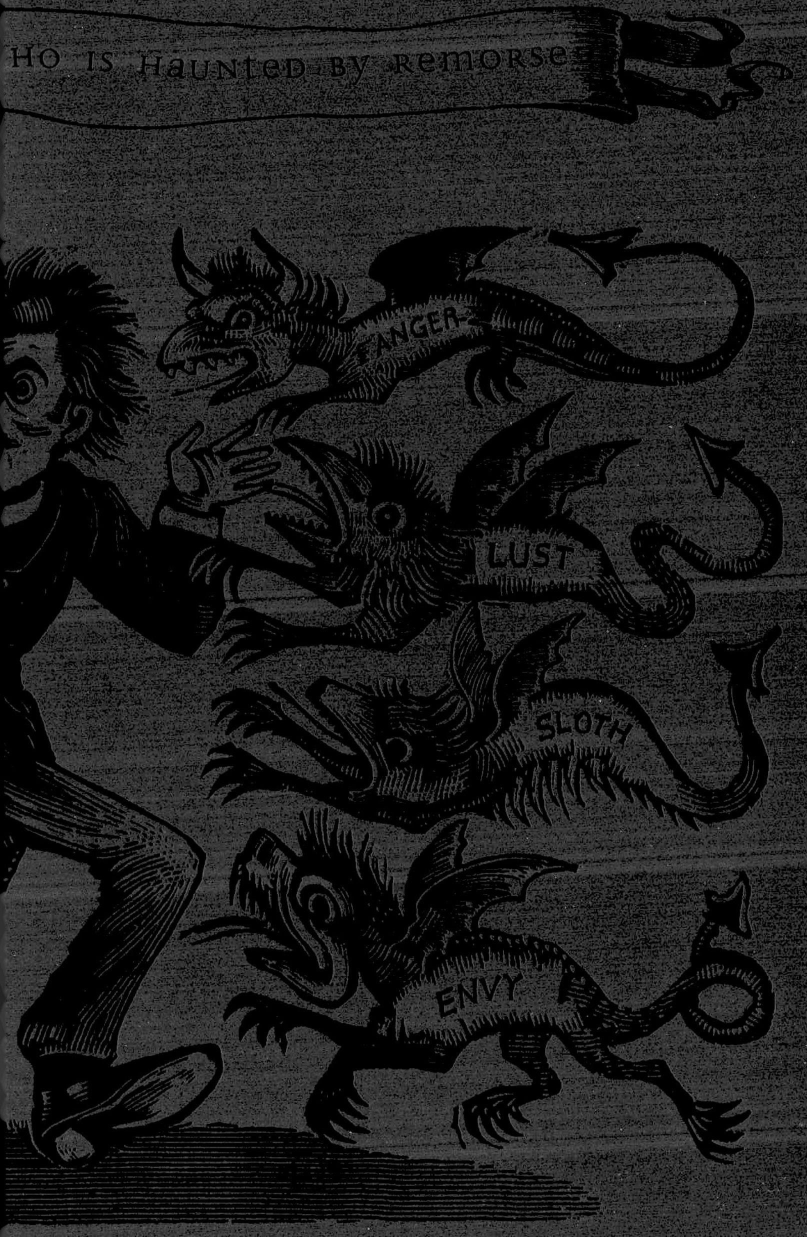
HO IS HAUNTED BY REMORSE
ANGER
LUST
SLOTH
ENVY

temptation and other games of fortune

Temptation comes in countless guises, but all temptation shares one lure—the occasional reward. My payoff rates are better than casinos or lottery tickets, and the fun I offer beats a day at the track!

We may say that between Lucifer and his servant a constant
hidden struggle goes on to find out who can deceive
the most ably. In truth, the Devil and the sorcerer never
play the game according to the rules.

MAURICE GARÇON AND JEAN VINCHON

poker faces

I watch for the revealing spark or gesture that settles the score, seals the contract. Simple business can be thrilling if you play it out right: the purchase of a carpet or a small piece of clothing, maybe some rare cologne or a delectable morsel. Or someone's soul, perhaps.

I most enjoy the moments immediately preceding the snag: those long, luscious seconds in which I entice my catch with an elegant lure. My senses sharpen. I dole out more bits of bait, watching as casual desire grows into a more insistent need.

Again, the devil taketh him up
into an exceeding high mountain, and sheweth him all the
kingdoms of the world, and the
glory of them; And saith unto
him, All these things will I give
thee, if thou wilt fall down and
worship me. Then saith Jesus
unto him, Get thee hence, Satan: for it is written, Thou shalt
worship the Lord thy God, and
him only shalt thou serve.

MATTHEW 4:8-10

Believe it if
you will.
But I tell this
story
differently…

Look at his expression!

He's been caught. *That's* why He looks embarrassed and guilty. You weren't supposed to see Him so tempted by my offers.

But temptation is splendid, really. The ability to be attracted, to consider, and then to choose is an attribute that distinguishes man from animal. He and His followers have never appreciated that aspect of the human psyche. For me, there is beauty in temptation, whereas I have never found glory in guilt.

Look at it another way. Who is more vile? A sleek preacher who tells you how wretchedly wicked you are? That your best days must be postponed until some promised future? Or an urbane, companionable gentleman who suggests that your finite days on this splendid planet are to be seized, savored, and thoroughly enjoyed? The choice is yours.

Hell now, Heaven later?
Heaven now, Heaven later?
Hell now, Hell later?
Heaven now, Hell later?
Heaven now, Hell never?
Hell now, Heaven never?
Hell never?

Dear Dr. Graham: What do you think is Satan's most effective method for getting people to follow his way instead of God? I guess that is a strange question, but I want to be on my guard against Satan and not be misled by what is wrong.   —Mrs. S. J.

Dear Mrs. S.J.: You are wise to be on guard against Satan, for he is real, and his one all-consuming goal is to work against God and what He wants to do in our lives.

Satan has all kinds of ways of working; the Bible even says that at times Satan "masquerades as an angel of light" (2 Corinthians 11:14). But his basic method does not change: He always seeks to exploit our weaknesses. If you have a problem with pride (for example), he will try to do things which appeal to your vanity and pride. If you have a problem with lust or greed or lying, he will do everything he can to exploit those, bringing across your path temptations that will appeal to that weakness.

But there are two truths to stress. First, Satan is a liar, and whatever he promises is a lie, "for there is not truth in him" (John 8:44). Second, Satan is a defeated foe. When Christ rose from the dead, He triumphed over sin and death and Satan—and some day His victory will be complete.

The way to resist Satan's power is to stay close to Christ. Have you opened your heart to Him, and are you seeking to follow Him? Focus on Christ, and let the truth of His Word, the Bible, guide you daily. "Be self-controlled and alert. Your enemy the devil prowls around like a roaring lion looking for someone to devour. Resist him, standing firm in the faith. . . . And the God of all grace . . . will himself restore you and make you strong, firm and steadfast" (1 Peter 5:8–10).

temptation, attraction,
and seduction

You can measure out time in many ways, but I like to look at life as one long string of temptations and seductions. As soon as you are old enough to make choices, you can be tempted. My perverse side admires the flagrant disregard with which a moth is drawn to a flame. (Can moths also be overcome with hubris?) That's a powerful attraction, but few humans feel so extreme an impulse, sparing themselves both pain and glory.

In fact, most humans agonize over smaller, more trivial matters. Should I eat this salad instead of that dessert? Should I listen to classical music or watch a soap opera on television? Should I read this important novel or that risqué magazine? Should I stay home with the family or go out for a drink?

You should know that I am not a player in mankind's every decision. Far from it; although for an admittedly cheap thrill, I do relish watching some overwrought creature wrestle his conscience to the dirt over a puny, inconsequential fret. As if I cared about his taste in food, television, companions, or erotica! Yet my affection for him is real: it is rooted in his quandary, his feeble rationalizations, and his guilt when he inevitably falls for the tawdry.

Like it or not, I am an addict who requires thrills of a specific magnitude. I invite you to imagine what they might be.

BUT temptation IS NOt
always a simple seduction

spare the rod,
spoil the demon

When pressed, even long-suffering Mary would resort to violence. She even spanked Jesus occasionally, a subject you'll never see on a church wall. He wasn't as easy a child to raise as you've been led to believe.

AN ODD ONE, WILLIAM BLAKE

His Job prints are magnificent. Good stubborn old Job.
Nothing could shake his faith, not pestilence, not boils,
not even his comforters. Ah, well.

   That's me in the trio above, with Sin and Death.
Even close friends can have misunderstandings.

GRANDIER, THE INQUISITION, AND THE DEVIL'S CHORD

Not all torture takes place in Hell, you know. Some of the most diabolical abuse has occurred within the confines of the Church. The Inquisition was no picnic for anyone whose notions of faith and worship deviated from the clergy's. If you enjoy nightmares, read the story of the handsome priest Urbain Grandier. The Church framed his problems as a battle between good and evil. You see here his "contract" with me. Actually, however, it was his talent with women in distress, particularly his dalliances with nuns, that was the cause of the trouble with his superiors. He was burned at the stake in 1634.

Today it is difficult to imagine how many aspects of life were dictated by Church doctrine. Music, for example, was shaped by theology, and a certain combination of musical notes was forbidden. The Devil's chord, "Diabolus in musica," was the name for that tritone. Considered evil and a means of conjuring me, this chord was banned for hundreds of years. Those caught playing it were tortured with implements of the day, including the skull crusher, wheel, and breast breaker.

I am fond of music and have inspired more than my share. My musical literature runs the gamut—and I am flattered. But it's the tritone I find irresistible, especially when played on the grand organ of Notre Dame!

You have the devil underrated:
I cannot yet persuaded be,
A fellow who is all behated
Must something be!

GOETHE

the Literary devil

The imagination is my guest room, and many writers have decorated it lavishly. My visits in fiction are usually more subtle and sometimes more profound than in the graphic arts. Could there be one single character in literature, sacred or profane, whose appearance has been more varied than mine? No. Certainly not.

Looks, behavior, and the right sense of style for each occasion are important, but achievement and influence are the ultimate measures of success. Taking the starring role in several masterpieces of Western literature is no mean feat.

Following are musings and a few selections on my protean nature. See for yourself how rich my literature is. I've relished all of my roles, whether as a noble creature or a party crasher. An incurably versatile actor am I.

CURIOUS DR. faust

I am perpetually astonished and amused by society's mistrust of intelligence. It works like this: If you are too smart for your times or your culture you must be possessed by the Devil. How else could you be so smart? Circular logic, a most popular kind.

Do not deny credit to the brain of man, which has evolved into a marvel of resilience and abstraction. No machine will ever equal the harmonic elegance of its cells, chemicals, hormones, and electrical pulses. What dreams it can create! What puzzles it can solve! But what terrifying suspicions it can conjure, too! I am not the first to suggest that the mind is the Devil and the Devil is in the mind. But even if that be true, what a marvelous possession is at your command. A waste not to take it for a quick spin or a long walk. (Didn't one of your pious politicians once remark that a mind is a terrible thing to lose? Wise man, he.)

The Church eternally wrestles with knotty problems created by the overuse of gray matter. (I doubt they are the best qualified to settle those disputes, but I admit to bias here.) In the thirteenth century, the brilliance of Thomas Aquinas helped the Church establish basic rules of intellectual order. His conclusion: Do what the Church tells you. Does this come as a surprise?

Blind faith or critical thought? Revelation or the scientific method? To remain satisfied with the apparent or to reach for the unknown? As long as brilliant minds continue to doubt doctrine—secular or sacred—such questions will lurk. These themes and others appear in the Faust stories, although they are handled differently by each author who wrestles with their riddles.

In the sixteenth century, the Church and heads of state throughout Europe were confronted with bright ideas and threatening achievements from clever imaginations outside their collective control. One such mind, that of Dr. Johannes Faust (a real-life wizard, physician, and alchemist) has for centuries since fascinated storytellers, dramatists, and composers: an august bunch that includes Christopher Marlowe, Johann von Goethe, Thomas Mann, Charles Gounod, Hector Berlioz, and Randy Newman. In Faust, readers and audiences have witnessed a brilliant mind struggling to reconcile the price and the value of knowledge. If you were Faust, what would you want to know and what would you be willing to trade for that knowledge?

maRKHeim

by ROBERT LOUIS STEVENSON

Markheim had just murdered a curio dealer and was looking for the key to the dealer's cabinet so he could steal his money, when he heard a step on the stair. He stood startled, yet transfixed, while the door opened and a face was thrust into the aperture, glanced round the room, looked at him, nodded and smiled as if in friendly recognition, and then withdrew again, and the door closed behind it. *After the door was closed, Markheim cried out in fright and the visitor returned.*

"Did you call me?" he asked, pleasantly, and with that he entered the room and closed the door behind him.

Markheim stood and gazed at him with all his eyes. Perhaps there was a film upon his sight, but the outlines of the newcomer seemed to change and waver like those of the idols in the wavering candlelight of the shop; and at times he thought he knew him; and at times he thought he bore a likeness to himself; and always, like a lump of living terror, there lay in his bosom the conviction that this thing was not of the earth and not of God.

And yet the creature had a strange air of the commonplace, as he stood looking on Markheim with a smile; and when he added: "You are looking for the money, I believe?" it was in the tones of everyday politeness.

Addressing Markheim by name, the stranger warned him that the dealer's maid would be back earlier than usual on this day and advised him to make his exit soon.

"You know me?" cried the murderer.

The visitor smiled. "You have long been a favorite of mine," he said; "and I have long observed and often sought to help you."

"What are you?" cried Markheim: "the devil?"

"What I may be," returned the other, "cannot affect the service I propose to render you."

"It can," cried Markheim, "it does! Be helped by you? No, never; not by you! You do not know me yet; thank God, you do not know me!"

"I know you," replied the visitant, with a sort of kind severity or rather firmness. "I know you to the soul."

Despite his many crimes, Markheim protested against this assertion. He claimed he could not be known by his actions because his heart was different from his actions. And, in any case, he said, this was his last crime, since he had decided to reform.

"You are to use this money on the Stock Exchange, I think?" remarked the visitor; "and there, if I mistake not, you have already lost some thousands?"

"Ah," said Markheim, "but this time I have a sure thing."

"This time, again, you will lose," replied the visitor quietly.

"Ah, but I keep back the half!" cried Markheim.

"That also you will lose," said the other.

Raising his finger, the stranger said, "For six-and-thirty years that you have been in this world . . . through many changes of fortune and varieties of humor, I have watched you steadily fall. Fifteen years ago you would have started at a theft. Three years back you would have blanched at the name of murder. Is there any crime, is there any cruelty or meanness, from which you still recoil?—five years from now I shall detect you in the fact! Downward, downward, lies your way; nor can anything but death avail to stop you."

Assuring Markheim that he would never change, the stranger advised him to kill the maid, who was outside ringing the doorbell. Do this, he told Markheim, and he would promise success.

But Markheim regarded his counselor with a steady eye. If he were truly evil, as the stranger had told him, he would rather lay down his life and place himself beyond the reach of all. For, said he, although "my love of good is damned to barrenness . . . I have still my hatred of evil; and from that, to your galling disappointment, you shall see that I can draw both energy and courage."

The features of the visitor began to undergo a wonderful and lovely change: they brightened and softened with a tender triumph; and, even as they brightened, faded and dislimned. But Markheim did not pause to watch or understand the transformation. *He went downstairs, greeted the maid with a smile, and told her to call for the police because he had just killed her master.*

That's how the devil is: how he is looking to you isn't how he is.
Your eyes see one thing while your heart is seeing another.

TOM SPANBAUER

tHe mysterious stranger

by MARK TWAIN

Soon there came a youth strolling toward us through the trees, and he sat down and began to talk in a friendly way, just as if he knew us. But we did not answer him, for he was a stranger and we were not used to strangers and were shy of them. He had new and good clothes on, and was handsome and had a winning face and a pleasant voice, and was easy and graceful and unembarrassed, not slouchy and awkward and diffident, like other boys. We wanted to be friendly with him, but didn't know how to begin. Then I thought of the pipe, and wondered if it would be taken as kindly meant if I offered it to him. But I remembered that we had no fire, so I was sorry and disappointed. But he looked up bright and pleased, and said:

"Fire? Oh, that is easy; I will furnish it."

I was so astonished I couldn't speak; for I had not said anything. He took the pipe and blew his breath on it, and the tobacco glowed red, and spirals of blue smoke rose up. We jumped up and were going to run, for that was natural; and we did run a few steps, although he was yearningly pleading for us to stay, and giving us his word that he would not do us any harm, but only wanted to be friends with us and have company. So we stopped and stood, and wanted to go back, being full of curiosity and wonder, but afraid to venture. He went on coaxing, in his soft, persuasive way; and when we saw that the pipe did not blow up and nothing happened, our confidence returned by little and little, and presently our curiosity got to be stronger than our fear, and we ventured back— but slowly, and ready to fly at any alarm.

He was bent on putting us at ease, and he had the right art; one could not remain doubtful and timorous where a person was so earnest and simple and gentle, and talked so alluringly as he did; no, he won us over, and it was not long before we were content and comfortable and chatty, and glad we had found this new friend. When the feeling of constraint was all gone we asked him how he had learned to do that strange thing, and he said he hadn't learned it at all; it came natural to him—like other things—other curious things.

"What ones?"

"Oh, a number; I don't know how many."

"Will you let us see you do them?"

"Do—please!" the others said.

"You won't run away again?"

"No—indeed we won't. Please do. Won't you?"

"Yes, with pleasure; but you mustn't forget your promise, you know."

We said we wouldn't, and he went to a puddle and came back with water in a cup which he had made out of a leaf, and blew upon it and threw it out, and it was a lump of ice the shape of the cup. We were astonished and charmed, but not afraid any more; we were very glad to be there, and asked him to go on and do some more things. And he did. He said he would give us any kind of fruit we liked, whether it was in season or not. We all spoke at once;

"Orange!"

"Apple!"

"Grapes!"

"They are in your pockets," he said, and it was true. And they were of the best, too, and we ate them and wished we had more, though none of us said so.

"You will find them where those came from," he said, "and everything else your appetites call for; and you need not name the thing you wish; as long as I am with you, you have only to wish and find."

And he said true. There was never anything so wonderful and so interesting. Bread, cakes, sweets, nuts—whatever one wanted, it was there. He ate nothing himself, but sat and chatted, and did one curious thing after another to amuse us. He made a tiny toy squirrel out of clay, and it ran up a tree and sat on a limb overhead and barked down at us. Then he made a dog that was not much larger than a mouse, and it treed the squirrel and danced about the tree, excited and barking, and was as alive as any dog could be. It frightened the squirrel from tree to tree and followed it up until both were out of sight in the forest. He made birds out of clay and set them free, and they flew away, singing.

At last I made bold to ask him to tell us who he was.

"An angel," he said, quite simply, and set another bird free and clapped his hands and made it fly away.

A kind of awe fell upon us when we heard him say that, and we were afraid again; but he said we need not be troubled, there was no occasion for us to be afraid of an angel, and he liked us, anyway. He went on chatting as simply and unaffectedly as ever; and while he talked he made a crowd of little men and women the size of your finger, and they went diligently to work and cleared and leveled off a space a couple of yards square in the grass and began to build a cunning little castle in it, the women mixing the mortar and carrying it up the scaffoldings in pails on their heads, just as our work-women have always done, and the men laying the courses of masonry—five hundred of these toy people swarming briskly about and working diligently and wiping the sweat off their faces as natural as life. In the absorbing interest of watching those five hundred little people make the castle grow step by step and course by course, and take shape and symmetry, that feeling and awe soon passed away and we were quite comfortable and at home again. We asked if we might make some people, and he said yes, and told Seppi to make some cannon for the walls, and told Nikolaus to make some halberdiers, with breastplates and greaves and helmets, and I was to make some cavalry, with horses, and in allotting these tasks he called us by our names, but did not say how he knew them. Then Seppi asked him what his own name was and he said, tranquilly, "Satan," and held out a chip and caught a little woman on it who was falling from the scaffolding and put her back where she belonged, and said, "She is an idiot to step backward like that and not notice what she is about."

It caught us suddenly, that name did, and our work dropped out of our hands and broke to pieces—a cannon, a halberdier, and a horse. Satan laughed, and asked what was the matter. I said, "Nothing, only it seemed a strange name for an angel." He asked why.

"Because it's—it's—well, it's his name, you know."

"Yes—he is my uncle."

He said it placidly, but it took our breath for a moment and made our hearts beat. He did not seem to notice that, but mended our halberdiers and things with a touch, handing them to us finished, and said, "Don't you remember?—he was an angel himself, once."

"Yes—it's true," said Seppi; "I didn't think of that."

"Before the Fall he was blameless."

"Yes," said Nikolaus, "he was without sin."

"It is a good family—ours," said Satan; "there is not a better. He is the only member of it that has ever sinned."

I should not be able to make any one understand how exciting it all was. You know that kind of quiver that trembles around through you when you are seeing something so strange and enchanting and wonderful that it is just a fearful joy to be alive and look at it; and you know how you gaze, and your lips turn dry and your breath comes short, but you wouldn't be anywhere but there, not for the world. I was bursting to ask one question—I had it on my tongue's end and could hardly hold it back—but I was ashamed to ask it; it might be a rudeness. Satan set an ox down that he had been making, and smiled up at me and said:

"It wouldn't be a rudeness, and I should forgive it if it was. Have I seen him? Millions of times. From the time that I was a little child a thousand years old I was his second favorite among the nursery angels of our blood and lineage—to use a human phrase —yes, from that time until the Fall, eight thousand years, measured as you count time."

"Eight—thousand!"

"Yes." He turned to Seppi, and went on as if answering something that was in Seppi's mind: "Why, naturally I look like a boy, for that is what I am. With us what you call time is a spacious thing; it takes a long stretch of it to grow an angel to full age." There was a question in my mind, and he turned to me and answered it, "I am sixteen thousand years old—counting as you count." Then he turned to Nikolaus and said: "No, the Fall did not affect me nor the rest of the relationship. It was only he that I was named for who ate of the fruit of the tree and then beguiled the man and the woman with it. We others are still ignorant of sin; we are not able to commit it; we are without blemish, and shall abide in that estate always. We—" Two of the little workmen were quarreling, and in buzzing little bumblebee voices they were cursing and swearing at each other; now came blows and blood; then they locked themselves together in a life-and-death struggle. Satan reached out his hand and crushed the life out of them with his fingers, threw them away, wiped the red from his fingers on his handkerchief, and went on talking where he had left off: "We cannot do wrong; neither have we any disposition to do it, for we do not know what it is."

It seemed a strange speech, in the circumstances, but we barely noticed that, we were so shocked and grieved at the wanton murder he had committed—for murder it was, that was its true name, and it was without palliation or excuse, for the men had not wronged him in any way. It made us miserable, for we loved him, and had thought him so noble and so beautiful and gracious, and had honestly believed he was an angel; and to have him do this cruel thing—ah, it lowered him so, and we had had such pride in him. He went right on talking, just as if nothing had happened, telling about his travels, and the interesting things he had seen in the big worlds of our solar systems and of other solar systems far away in the remotenesses of space, and about the customs of the immortals that inhabit them, somehow fascinating us, enchanting us, charming us in spite of the pitiful scene that was now under our eyes, for the wives of the little dead men had found the crushed and shapeless bodies and were crying over them, and sobbing and lamenting, and a priest was kneeling there with his hands crossed upon his breast, praying; and crowds and crowds of pitying friends were massed about them, reverently uncovered, with their bare heads bowed, and many with the tears running down—a scene which Satan paid no attention to until the small noise of the weeping and praying began to annoy him, then he reached out and took the heavy board seat out of our swing and brought it down and mashed all those people into the earth just as if they had been flies, and went on talking just the same.

An angel, and kill a priest! An angel who did not know how to do wrong, and yet destroys in cold blood hundreds of helpless poor men and women who had never done him any harm! It made us sick to see that awful deed, and to think that none of those poor creatures was prepared except the priest, for none of them had ever heard a mass or seen a church. And we were witnesses; we had seen these murders done and it was our duty to tell, and let the law take its course.

But he went on talking right along, and worked his enchantments upon us again with that fatal music of his voice. He made us forget everything; we could only listen to him, and love him, and be his slaves, to do with us as he would. He made us drunk with the joy of being with him, and of looking into the heaven of his eyes, and of feeling the ecstasy that thrilled along our veins from the touch of his hand.

The Stranger had seen everything, he had been everywhere, he knew everything, and he forgot nothing. What another must study, he learned at a glance; there were no difficulties for him. And he made things live before you when he told about them. He saw the world made; he saw Adam created; he saw Samson surge against the pillars and bring the temple down in ruins about him; he saw Caesar's death; he told of the daily life in heaven; he had seen the damned writhing in the red waves of hell; and he made us see all these things, and it was as if we were on the spot and looking at them with our own eyes. And we felt them, too, but there was no sign that they were anything to him beyond mere entertainments. Those visions of hell, those poor babes and women and girls and lads and men shrieking and supplicating in anguish—why, we could hardly bear it, but he was as bland about it as if it had been so many imitation rats in an artificial fire.

And always when he was talking about men and women here on the earth and their doings—even their grandest and sublimest —we were secretly ashamed, for his manner showed that to him they and their doings were of paltry poor consequence; often you would think he was talking about flies, if you didn't know. Once he even said, in so many words, that our people down here were quite interesting to him, notwithstanding they were so dull and ignorant and trivial and conceited, and so diseased and rickety, and such a shabby, poor, worthless lot all around. He said it in a quite matter-of-course way and without bitterness, just as a person might talk about bricks or manure or any other thing that was of no consequence and hadn't feelings. I could see he meant no offense, but in my thoughts I set it down as not very good manners.

"Manners!" he said. "Why, it is merely the truth, and truth is good manners; manners are a fiction. The castle is done. Do you like it?"

Any one would have been obliged to like it. It was lovely to look at, it was so shapely and fine, and so cunningly perfect in all its particulars, even to the little flags waving from the turrets. Satan said we must put the artillery in place now, and station the halberdiers and display the cavalry. Our men and horses were a spectacle to see, they were so little like what they were intended for; for, of course, we had no art in making such things. Satan said they were the worst he had seen; and when he touched them and made them alive, it was just ridiculous the way they acted, on account of their legs not being of uniform lengths. They reeled and sprawled around as if they were drunk, and endangered everybody's lives around them, and finally fell over and lay helpless and kicking. It made us all laugh, though it was a shameful thing to see. The guns were charged with dirt, to fire a salute, but they were so crooked and so badly made that they all burst when they went off, and killed some of the gunners and crippled the others. Satan said we would have a storm now, and an earthquake, if we liked, but we must stand off a piece, out of danger. We wanted to call the people away, too, but he said never mind them; they were of no consequence, and we could make more, some time or other, if we needed them.

A small storm-cloud began to settle down black over the castle, and the miniature lightning and thunder began to play, and the ground to quiver, and the wind to pipe and wheeze, and the rain to fall, and all the people flocked into the castle for shelter. The cloud settled down blacker and blacker, and one could see the castle only dimly through it; the lightning blazed out flash upon flash and pierced the castle and set it on fire, and the flames shone out red and fierce through the cloud, and the people came flying out, shrieking, but Satan brushed them back, paying no attention to our begging and crying and imploring; and in the midst of the howling of the wind and volleying of the thunder the magazine blew up, the earthquake rent the ground wide, and the castle's wreck and ruin tumbled into the chasm, which swallowed it from sight, and closed upon it, with all that innocent life, not one of the five hundred poor creatures escaping. Our hearts were broken; we could not keep from crying.

"Don't cry," Satan said; "they were of no value."

"But they are gone to hell!"

"Oh, it is no matter; we can make plenty more."

It was of no use to try to move him; evidently he was wholly without feeling, and could not understand. He was full of bubbling spirits, and as gay as if this were a wedding instead of a fiendish massacre. And he was bent on making us feel as he did, and of course his magic accomplished his desire. It was no trouble to him; he did whatever he pleased with us. In a little while we were dancing on that grave, and he was playing to us on a strange, sweet instrument which he took out of his pocket; and the music—but there is no music like that, unless perhaps in heaven, and that was where he brought it from, he said. It made one mad, for pleasure; and we could not take our eyes from him, and the looks that went out of our eyes came from our hearts, and their dumb speech was worship. He brought the dance from heaven, too, and the bliss of paradise was in it.

Presently he said he must go away on an errand. But we could not bear the thought of it, and clung to him, and pleaded with him to stay; and that pleased him, and he said so, and said he would not go yet, but would wait a little while and we would sit down and talk a few minutes longer; and he told us Satan was only his real name, and he was to be known by it to us alone, but he had chosen another one to be called by in the presence of others; just a common one, such as people have—Philip Traum.

It sounded so odd and mean for such a being! But it was his decision, and we said nothing; his decision was sufficient.

We had seen wonders this day; and my thoughts began to run on the pleasure it would be to tell them when I got home, but he noticed those thoughts, and said:

"No, all these matters are a secret among us four. I do not mind your trying to tell them, if you like, but I will protect your tongues, and nothing of the secret will escape from them."

The hall door opened and in came the pilgrim. God knows what manner of man he was; I cannot tell you. He certainly was lean and lithe like a cat, his eyes danced in his head like the very devil, but his cheeks and jaws were as bare of flesh as any hermit's that lives on roots and ditchwater. His yellow-hosed legs went like the tune of a May game, and he screwed and twisted his scarlet-jerkined body in time with them. In his left hand he held a cithern, on which he twanged with his right, making a cunning noise that titillated the backbones of those who heard it, and teased every delicate nerve in the body. Such a tune would have tickled the ribs of Death himself. A queer fellow to go pilgrimaging certainly, but why, when they saw him, all the young nuns tittered and the old nuns grinned, until they showed their red gums, it is hard to tell. Even the Lady Mother on the dais smiled, though she tried to frown a moment later.

FRANCIS OSCAR MANN
from *The Devil in a Nunnery*

tHe painteR's baRÇaiN

by WILLIAM THACKERAY

"You were just speaking of me," said the voice.

Gambouge held, in his left hand, his palette; in his right, a bladder of crimson lake, which he was about to squeeze out upon the mahogany. "Where are you?" cried he again.

"S-q-u-e-e-z-e!" exclaimed the little voice.

Gambouge picked out the nail from the bladder, and gave a squeeze; when, as sure as I'm living, a little imp spurted out from the hole upon the palette, and began laughing in the most singular and oily manner.

When first born he was little bigger than a tadpole; then he grew to be as big as a mouse; then he arrived at the size of a cat; and then he jumped off the palette, and, turning head over heels, asked the poor painter what he wanted with him. *And so did the little imp incarnate into his true self, Diabolus, before the very eyes of Gambouge the painter.*

Gambouge, much in want of wealth, entered into a pact with Diabolus: He was to have all he wished for seven years, and at the end of that time was to become the property of the [Devil]; provided that during the course of the seven years, every single wish which he might form should be gratified by the other of the contracting parties; otherwise the deed became null and nonavenue, and Gambouge should be left "to go to the [devil] his own way."

For six years and six months their contract had endured, when a sudden and desperate resolution seemed all at once to have taken possession of Simon Gambouge. *And so he gathered together all of his family and friends for a sumptuous feast.*

After dinner, using the customary formula, he called upon Diabolus to appear. The old ladies screamed and hoped he would not appear naked; the young ones tittered, and longed to see the monster: everybody was pale with expectation and affright.

A very quiet, gentlemanly man, neatly dressed in black, made his appearance, to the surprise of all present, and bowed all round to the company. "I will not show my *credentials*," he said, blushing and pointing to his hoofs, which were cleverly hidden by his pumps and shoe-buckles, "unless the ladies absolutely wish it; but I am the person you want."

Simon Gambouge then proffered to Diabolus his odious wife, Griskinissa Gambouge, from whom he had long desired to extricate himself. "Live alone with her for half a year," *he said,* "never leave her from morning till night, ... and listen to all the abuse which falls from her infernal tongue. Do this, and I ask no more of you; I will deliver myself up at the appointed time."

The Devil, at this, grinned so horribly that every drop of beer in the house turned sour: he gnashed his teeth so frightfully that every person in the company wellnigh fainted with the cholic. He slapped down the great parchment upon the floor, trampled upon it madly, and lashed it with his hoofs and his tail: at last, spreading out a mighty pair of wings as wide as from here to Regent Street, he slapped Gambouge with his tail over one eye, and vanished, abruptly, through the key-hole.

His countenance was of a dark snuff-color, and he had a long hooked nose, pea eyes, a wide mouth, and an excellent set of teeth, which latter he seemed anxious of displaying, as he was grinning from ear to ear. What with mustachios and whiskers, there was none of the rest of his face to be seen. His head was uncovered, and his hair neatly done up in *papillotes*. His dress was a tight-fitting swallow-tailed black coat (from one of whose pockets dangled a vast length of white handkerchief), black kerseymere knee-breeches, black stockings, and stumpy-looking pumps, with huge bunches of black satin ribbon for bows. Under one arm he carried a huge *chapeau-de-bras*, and under the other a fiddle nearly five times as big as himself. In his left hand was a gold snuff-box, from which, as he capered down the hill, cutting all manner of fantastic steps, he took snuff incessantly with an air of the greatest possible self-satisfaction.

EDGAR ALLAN POE
from *The Devil in the Belfry*

BON - BON

by EDGAR ALLAN POE

The philosopher's amazement did not prevent a narrow scrutiny of
the stranger's dress and appearance. The outlines of his figure, ex-
ceedingly lean, but much above the common height, were rendered
minutely distinct by means of a faded suit of black cloth which fit-
ted tight to the skin, but was otherwise cut very much in the style
of a century ago. These garments had evidently been intended for
a much shorter person than their present owner. His ankles and
wrists were left naked for several inches. In his shoes, however, a
pair of very brilliant buckles gave the lie to the extreme poverty implied by the other portions of his dress. His head was bare, and
entirely bald, with the exception of the hinderpart, from which depended a *queue* of considerable length. A pair of green spectacles,
with side glasses, protected his eyes from the influence of the light,
and at the same time prevented our hero from ascertaining either
their colour or their conformation. About the entire person there
was no evidence of a shirt; but a white cravat, of filthy appearance,
was tied with extreme precision around the throat, and the ends,
hanging down formally side by side gave (although I dare say unin-
tentionally) the idea of an ecclesiastic. Indeed, many other points
both in his appearance and demeanour might have very well sus-
tained a conception of that nature. Over his left ear, he carried, after the fashion of a modern clerk, an instrument resembling the
stylus of the ancients. In a breast-pocket of his coat appeared con-
spicuously a small black volume fastened with clasps of steel. This
book, whether accidentally or not, was so turned outwardly from

the person as to discover the words *"Rituel Catholique"* in white letters upon the back. His entire physiognomy was interestingly saturnine—even cadaverously pale. The forehead was lofty, and deeply furrowed with the ridges of contemplation. The corners of the mouth were drawn down into an expression of the most submissive humility. There was also a clasping of the hands, as he stepped towards our hero—a deep sigh—and altogether a look of such utter sanctity as could not have failed to be unequivocally prepossessing. . . .

It was impossible that so accurate an observer of men and things [as the philosopher] should have failed to discover, upon the moment, the real character of the personage who had thus intruded upon his hospitality. To say no more, the conformation of his visitor's feet was sufficiently remarkable—he maintained lightly upon his head an inordinately tall hat—there was a tremulous swelling about the hinder-part of his breeches—and the vibration of his coat tail was a palpable fact. . . .

"I see you know me, Bon-Bon," said he. . . .

"Why, sir," said the philosopher, "why, sir, to speak sincerely —I believe you are—upon my word . . . that is to say, I think—I imagine . . ."

"Oh!—ah!—yes!—very well!" interrupted his Majesty; "say no more—I see how it is." And hereupon, taking off his green spectacles, he wiped the glasses carefully with the sleeve of his coat, and deposited them in his pocket.

If Bon-Bon had been astonished at the incident of the book, his amazement was now much increased by the spectacle which here presented itself to view. In raising his eyes, with a strong feeling of curiosity to ascertain the colour of his guest's, he found them by no means black, as he had anticipated—nor grey, as might have been imagined—nor yet hazel nor blue—nor indeed yellow nor red—nor purple—nor white—nor green—nor any other colour in the heavens above, or in the earth beneath, or in the waters under the earth. In short, Pierre Bon-Bon not only saw plainly that his Majesty had no eyes whatsoever, but could discover no indications of their having existed at any previous period—for the space where eyes should naturally have been was, I am constrained to say, simply a dead level of flesh.

I

From his brimstone bed at break of day
A walking the Devil is gone,
To visit his snug little farm the Earth,
And see how his stock goes on.

II

Over the hill and over the dale,
And he went over the plain,
And backward and forward he switched his long tail
As a gentleman switches his cane.

III

And how then was the Devil drest?
Oh! he was in his Sunday's best:
His jacket was red and his breeches were blue,
And there was a hole where the tail came through.

SAMUEL TAYLOR COLERIDGE
from *The Devil's Thoughts*

the
generous gambler

by charles baudelaire

Yesterday, across the crowd of the boulevard, I found myself touched by a mysterious Being I had always desired to know, and who I recognized immediately, in spite of the fact that I had never seen him. He had, I imagined, in himself, relatively as to me, a similar desire, for he gave me, in passing, so significant a sign in his eyes that I hastened to obey him. I followed him attentively, and soon I descended behind him into a subterranean dwelling, astonishing to me as a vision, where shone a luxury of which none of the actual houses in Paris could give me an approximate example. It seemed to me singular that I had passed so often that prodigious retreat without having discovered the entrance. There reigned an exquisite, an almost stifling atmosphere, which made one forget almost instantaneously all the fastidious horrors of life; there I breathed a sombre sensuality, like that of opium-smokers when, set on the shore of an enchanted island, over which shone an eternal afternoon, they felt born in them, to the soothing sounds of melodious cascades, the desire of never again seeing their households, their women, their children, and of never again being tossed on the decks of ships by storms.

There were there strange faces of men and women, gifted with so fatal a beauty that I seemed to have seen them years ago and in countries which I failed to remember, and which inspired in me that curious sympathy and that equally curious sense of fear that I usually discover in unknown aspects. If I wanted to define in some fashion or other the singular expression of their eyes, I would say that never had I seen such magic radiance more energetically expressing the horror of *ennui* and of desire—of the immortal desire of feeling themselves alive.

As for mine host and myself, we were already, as we sat down, as perfect friends as if we had always known each other. We drank immeasurably of all sorts of extraordinary wines, and—a thing not less bizarre—it seemed to me, after several hours, that I was no more intoxicated than he was.

However, gambling, this superhuman pleasure, had cut, at various intervals, our copious libations, and I ought to say that I had gained and lost my soul, as we were playing, with an heroical carelessness and lightheartedness. The soul is so invisible a thing, often useless and sometimes so troublesome, that I did not experience, as to this loss, more than that kind of emotion I might have, had I lost my visiting card in the street.

We spent hours in smoking cigars, whose incomparable savour and perfume give to the soul the nostalgia of unknown delights and sights, and, intoxicated by all these spiced sauces, I dared, in an access of familiarity which did not seem to displease him, to cry, as I lifted a glass filled to the brim with wine: "To your immortal health, Old He-Goat!"

We talked of the universe, of its creation and of its future destruction; of the leading ideas of the century—that is to say, of Progress and Perfectibility—and, in general, of all kinds of human infatuations. On this subject his Highness was inexhaustible in his irrefutable jests, and he expressed himself with a splendour of diction and with a magnificence in drollery such as I have never found in any of the most famous conversationalists of our age. He explained to me the absurdity of different philosophies that had so far taken possession of men's brains, and deigned even to take me in confidence in regard to certain fundamental principles, which I am not inclined to share with any one.

He complained in no way of the evil reputation under which he lived, indeed, all over the world, and he assured me that he himself was of all living beings the most interested in the destruction of *Superstition*, and he avowed to me that he had been afraid, relatively as to his proper power, once only, and that was on the day when he had heard a preacher, more subtle than the rest of the human herd, cry in his pulpit: "My dear brethren, do not ever forget, when you hear the progress of lights praised, that the loveliest trick of the Devil is to persuade you that he does not exist!"

The memory of this famous orator brought us naturally on the subject of Academies, and my strange host declared to me that he didn't disdain, in many cases, to inspire the pens, the words, and the consciences of pedagogues, and that he almost always assisted in person, in spite of being invisible, at all the scientific meetings.

Encouraged by so much kindness I asked him if he had any news of God—who has not his hours of impiety?—especially as the old friend of the Devil. He said to me, with a shade of unconcern united with a deeper shade of sadness: "We salute each other when we meet." But, for the rest, he spoke in Hebrew.

It is uncertain if his Highness has ever given so long an audience to a simple mortal, and I feared to abuse it.

Finally, as the dark approached shivering, this famous personage, sung by so many poets, and served by so many philosophers who work for his glory's sake without being aware of it, said to me: "I want you to remember me always, and to prove to you that I—of whom one says so much evil—am often enough *bon diable*, to make use of one of your vulgar locutions. So as to make up for the irremediable loss that you have made of your soul, I shall give you back the stake you ought to have gained, if your fate had been fortunate—that is to say, the possibility of solacing and of conquering, during your whole life, this bizarre affection of *ennui*, which is the source of all your maladies and of all your miseries. Never a desire shall be formed by you that I will not aid you to realize; you will reign over your vulgar equals; money and gold and diamonds, fairy palaces, shall come to seek you and shall ask you to accept them without your having made the least effort to obtain them;

you can change your abode as often as you like; you shall have in your power all sensualities without lassitude, in lands where the climate is always hot, and where the women are as scented as the flowers." With this he rose up and said good-bye to me with a charming smile.

If it had not been for the shame of humiliating myself before so immense an assembly, I might have voluntarily fallen at the feet of this generous Gambler, to thank him for his unheard-of munificence. But, little by little, after I had left him, an incurable defiance entered into me; I dared no longer believe in so prodigious a happiness; and as I went to bed, making over again my nightly prayer by means of all that remained in me in the matter of faith, I repeated in my slumber: "My God, my Lord, My God! Do let the Devil keep his word with me!"

a nursery tale

by VLADIMIR NABOKOV

1

Fantasy, the flutter, the rapture of fantasy! Erwin knew these things well. In a tram, he would always sit on the right-hand side, so as to be nearer the sidewalk. Twice daily, from the tram he took to the office and back, Erwin looked out of the window and collected his harem. Happy, happy Erwin, to dwell in such a convenient, such a fairy-tale German town!

He covered one sidewalk in the morning, on his way to work, and the other in the late afternoon, on his way home. First one, then the other was bathed in voluptuous sunlight, for the sun also went and returned. We should bear in mind that Erwin was so morbidly shy that only once in his life, taunted by rascally comrades, he had accosted a woman, and she had said quietly: "You ought to be ashamed of yourself. Leave me alone." Thereafter, he had avoided conversation with strange young ladies. In compensation, separated from the street by a windowpane, clutching to his ribs a black briefcase, wearing scuffed trousers with a pinstripe, and stretching one leg under the opposite seat (if unoccupied), Erwin looked boldly and freely at passing girls, and then would suddenly bite his nether lip: this signified the capture of a new concubine; whereupon he would set her aside, as it were, and his swift gaze, jumping like a compass needle, was already seeking out the next one. Those beauties were far from him, and therefore the sweetness of free choice could not be affected by sullen timidity. If, however, a girl happened to sit down across from him, and a certain twinge told him that she was pretty, he would retract his leg from under her seat with all the signs of a gruffness quite uncharacteristic of his young age—and could not bring himself to take stock of her: the bones of his forehead—right here, over the eyebrows—ached from shyness, as if an iron helmet were restricting his temples and preventing him from raising his eyes; and what a relief it was when she got up and went toward the exit. Then, feigning casual abstraction, he looked—shameless Erwin did look—following her receding back, swallowing whole her adorable nape and silk-hosed calves, and thus, after all, would he add her to his fabulous harem! The leg would again be stretched, again the bright sidewalk would flow past the window, and again, his thin pale nose with a noticeable depression at the tip directed streetward, Erwin would accumulate his slave girls. And this is fantasy, the flutter, the rapture of fantasy!

2

One Saturday, on a frivolous evening in May, Erwin was sitting at a sidewalk table. He watched the tripping throng of the avenue, now and then biting his lip with a quick incisor. The entire sky was tinged with pink and the streetlamps and shop-sign bulbs glowed with a kind of unearthly light in the gathering dusk. The first lilacs were being hawked by an anemic but pretty young girl. Rather fittingly the café phonograph was singing the Flower Aria from *Faust*.

A tall middle-aged lady in a charcoal tailor-made suit, heavily, yet not ungracefully, swinging her hips, made her way among the sidewalk tables. There was no vacant one. Finally, she put one hand in a glossy black glove upon the back of the empty chair opposite Erwin.

"May I?" queried her unsmiling eyes from under the short veil of her velvet hat.

"Yes, certainly," answered Erwin, slightly rising and ducking. He was not awed by such solid-built women with thickly powdered, somewhat masculine jowls.

Down onto the table with a resolute thud went her oversize

handbag. She ordered a cup of coffee and a wedge of apple tart. Her deep voice was somewhat hoarse but pleasant.

The vast sky, suffused with dull rose, grew darker. A tram screeched by, inundating the asphalt with the radiant tears of its lights. And short-skirted beauties walked by. Erwin's glance followed them.

I want this one, he thought, noticing his nether lip. And that one, too.

"I think it could be arranged," said his vis-à-vis in the same calm husky tones in which she had addressed the waiter.

Erwin almost fell off his chair. The lady looked intently at him, as she pulled off one glove to tackle her coffee. Her made-up eyes shone cold and hard, like showy false jewels. Dark pouches swelled under them, and—what seldom occurs in the case of women, even elderly women—hairs grew out of her feline-shaped nostrils. The shed glove revealed a big wrinkled hand with long, convex, beautiful fingernails.

"Don't be surprised," she said with a wry smile. She muffled a yawn and added: "In point of fact, I am the Devil."

Shy, naive Erwin took this to be a figure of speech, but the lady, lowering her voice, continued as follows:

"Those who imagine me with horns and a thick tail are greatly mistaken. Only once did I appear in that shape, to some Byzantine imbecile, and I really don't know why it was such a damned success. I am born three or four times every two centuries. In the eighteen-seventies, some fifty years ago, I was buried, with picturesque honors and a great shedding of blood, on a hill above a cluster of African villages of which I had been ruler. My term there was a rest after more stringent incarnations. Now I am a German-born woman whose last husband—I had, I think, three in all—was of French extraction, a Professor Monde. In recent years I have driven several young men to suicide, caused a well-known artist to copy and multiply the picture of the Westminster Abbey on the pound note, incited a virtuous family man—But there is really nothing to brag about. This has been a pretty banal avatar, and I am fed up with it."

She gobbled up her slice of tart and Erwin, mumbling something, reached for his hat, which had fallen under the table.

"No, don't go yet," said Frau Monde, simultaneously beckoning the waiter. "I am offering you something. I am offering you a harem. And if you are still skeptical of my power—See that old gentleman in tortoiseshell glasses crossing the street? Let's have him hit by a tram."

Erwin, blinking, turned streetward. As the old man reached the tracks he took out his handkerchief and was about to sneeze into it. At the same instant, a tram flashed, screeched, and rolled past. From both sides of the avenue people rushed toward the tracks. The old gentleman, his glasses and handkerchief gone, was sitting on the asphalt. Someone helped him up. He stood, sheepishly shaking his head, brushing his coat sleeves with the palms of his hands, and wiggling one leg to test its condition.

"I said 'hit by a tram,' not 'run over,' which I might also have said," remarked Frau Monde coolly, as she worked a thick cigarette into an enameled holder. "In any case, this is an example."

She blew two streams of gray smoke through her nostrils and again fixed Erwin with her hard bright eyes.

"I liked you immediately. That shyness, that bold imagination. You reminded me of an innocent, though hugely endowed, young monk whom I knew in Tuscany. This is my penultimate night. Being a woman has its points, but being an aging woman is hell, if you will pardon me the expression. Moreover, I made such mischief the other day—you will soon read about it in all the papers—that I had better get out of this life. Next Monday I plan to be born elsewhere. The Siberian slut I have chosen shall be the mother of a marvelous, monstrous man."

"I see," said Erwin.

"Well, my dear boy," continued Frau Monde, demolishing her second piece of pastry, "I intend, before going, to have a bit of innocent fun. Here is what I suggest. Tomorrow, from noon to midnight you can select by your usual method" (with heavy humor Frau Monde sucked in her lower lip with a succulent hiss) "all the girls you fancy. Before my departure, I shall have them gathered and placed at your complete disposal. You will keep them until you have enjoyed them all. How does that strike you, *amico?*"

Erwin dropped his eyes and said softly: "If it is all true, it would be a great happiness."

"All right then," she said, and licked the remains of whipped cream off her spoon: "All right. One condition, nevertheless, must be set. No, it is not what you are thinking. As I told you, I have arranged my next incarnation. Your soul I do not require. Now this is the condition: the total of your choices between noon and midnight must be an odd number. This is essential and final. Otherwise I can do nothing for you."

Erwin cleared his throat and asked, almost in a whisper: "How shall I know? Let's say I've chosen one—what then?"

"Nothing," said Frau Monde. "Your feeling, your desire, are a command in themselves. However, in order that you may be sure that the deal stands, I shall have a sign given you every time—a smile, not necessarily addressed to you, a chance word in the crowd, a sudden patch of color—that sort of thing. Don't worry, you'll know."

"And—and—" mumbled Erwin, shuffling his feet under the table: "—and where is it all going to—uh—happen? I have only a very small room."

"Don't worry about that either," said Frau Monde, and her corset creaked as she rose. "Now it's time you went home. No harm in getting a good night's rest. I'll give you a lift."

In the open taxi, with the dark wind streaming between starry sky and glistening asphalt, poor Erwin felt tremendously elated.

Frau Monde sat erect, her crossed legs forming a sharp angle, and the city lights flashed in her gemlike eyes.

"Here's your house," she said, touching Erwin's shoulder. "*Au revoir.*"

<h1 style="text-align:center">3</h1>

Many are the dreams that can be brought on by a mug of dark beer laced with brandy. Thus reflected Erwin when he awoke the next morning—he must have been drunk, and the talk with that funny female was all fancy. This rhetorical turn often occurs in fairy tales and, as in fairy tales, our young man soon realized he was wrong.

He went out just as the church clock had begun the laborious task of striking noon. Sunday bells joined in excitedly, and a bright breeze ruffled the Persian lilacs around the public lavatory in the small park near his house. Pigeons settled on an old stone *Herzog* or waddled along the sandbox where little children, their flannel behinds sticking up, were digging with toy scoops and playing with wooden trains. The lustrous leaves of the lindens moved in the wind; their ace-of-spades shadows quivered on the graveled path and climbed in an airy flock the trouser legs and skirts of the strollers, racing up and scattering over shoulders and faces, and once again the whole flock slipped back onto the ground, where, barely stirring, they lay in wait for the next foot passenger. In this variegated setting, Erwin noticed a girl in a white dress who had squatted down to tousle with two fingers a fat shaggy pup with warts on its belly. The inclination of her head bared the back of her neck, revealing the ripple of her vertebrae, the fair bloom, the tender hollow between her shoulder blades, and the sun through the leaves found fiery strands in her chestnut hair. Still playing with the puppy, she half-rose from her haunches and clapped her hands above it. The fat little animal rolled over on the gravel, ran off a few feet, and toppled on its side. Erwin sat down on a bench and cast a timid and avid glance at her face.

He saw her so clearly, with such piercing and perfect force of perception, that, it seemed, nothing new about her features might have been disclosed by years of previous intimacy. Her palish lips twitched as if repeating every small soft movement of the puppy; her eyelashes beat so brightly as to look like the raylets of her beaming eyes; but most enchanting, perhaps, was the curve of her cheek, now slightly in profile; that dipping line no words, of course, could describe. She started running, showing nice legs, and the puppy tumbled in her wake like a woolly ball. In sudden awareness of his miraculous might, Erwin caught his breath and awaited the promised signal. At that moment the girl turned her head as she ran and flashed a smile at the plump little creature that could barely keep up with her.

"Number one," Erwin said to himself with unwonted complacency, and got up from his bench.

He followed the graveled path with scraping footsteps, in gaudy, reddish-yellow shoes worn only on Sundays. He left the oasis of the diminutive park and crossed over to Amadeus Boulevard. Did his eyes rove? Oh, they did. But, maybe, because the girl in white had somehow left a sunnier mark than any remembered impression, some dancing blind spot prevented him from finding another sweetheart. Soon, however, the blot dissolved, and near a glazed pillar with the tramway timetable our friend observed two young ladies—sisters, or even twins, to judge by their striking resemblance—who were discussing a streetcar route in vibrant, echoing voices. Both were small and slim, dressed in black silk, with saucy eyes and painted lips.

"That's exactly the tram you want," one of them kept saying.

"Both, please," Erwin requested quickly.

"Yes, of course," said the other in response to her sister's words.

Erwin continued along the boulevard. He knew all the smart streets where the best possibilities existed.

"Three," he said to himself. "Odd number. So far so good. And if it were midnight right now—"

Swinging her handbag she was coming down the steps of the Leilla, one of the best local hotels. Her big blue-chinned companion slowed down behind her to light his cigar. The lady was lovely, hatless, bobhaired, with a fringe on her forehead that made her look like a boy actor in the part of a damsel. As she went by, now closely escorted by our ridiculous rival, Erwin remarked simultaneously the crimson artificial rose in the lapel of her jacket and the advertisement on a billboard: a blond-mustachioed Turk and, in large letters, the word "YES!," under which it said in smaller characters: "I SMOKE ONLY THE ROSE OF THE ORIENT."

That made four, divisible by two, and Erwin felt eager to restore the odd-number rigmarole without delay. In a lane off the boulevard there was a cheap restaurant which he sometimes frequented on Sundays when sick of his landlady's fare. Among the girls he had happened to note at one time or another there had been a wench who worked in that place. He entered and ordered his favorite dish: blood sausage and sauerkraut. His table was next to the telephone. A man in a bowler called a number and started to jabber as ardently as a hound that has picked up the scent of a hare. Erwin's glance wandered toward the bar—and there was the girl he had seen three or four times before. She was beautiful in a drab, freckled way, if beauty can be drably russet. As she raised her bare arms to place her washed beer steins he saw the red tufts of her armpits.

"All right, all right!" barked the man into the mouthpiece.

With a sigh of relief enriched by a belch, Erwin left the restaurant. He felt heavy and in need of a nap. To tell the truth, the new shoes pinched like crabs. The weather had changed. The air was sultry. Great domed clouds grew and crowded one another in the hot sky. The streets were becoming deserted. One could feel the houses fill to the brim with Sunday-afternoon snores. Erwin boarded a streetcar.

The tram started to roll. Erwin turned his pale face, shining with sweat, to the window, but no girls walked. While paying his fare he noticed, on the other side of the aisle, a woman sitting with her back to him. She wore a black velvet hat, and a light frock patterned with intertwined chrysanthemums against a semitransparent mauve background through which showed the shoulder straps of her slip. The lady's statuesque bulk made Erwin curious to glimpse her face. When her hat moved and, like a black ship, started to turn, he first looked away as usual, glanced in feigned abstraction at a youth sitting opposite him, at his own fingernails, at a red-cheeked little old man dozing in the rear of the car, and, having thus established a point of departure justifying further castings-around, Erwin shifted his casual gaze to the lady now looking his way. It was Frau Monde. Her full, no-longer-young face was blotchily flushed from the heat, her mannish eyebrows bristled above her piercing prismatic eyes, a slightly sardonic smile curled up the corners of her compressed lips.

"Good afternoon," she said in her soft husky voice: "Come sit over here. Now we can have a chat. How are things going?"

"Only five," replied Erwin with embarrassment.

"Excellent. An odd number. I would advise you to stop there. And at midnight—ah, yes, I don't think I told you—at midnight you are to come to Hoffmann Street. Know where that is? Look between Number Twelve and Fourteen. The vacant lot there will be replaced by a villa with a walled garden. The girls of your choice will be waiting for you on cushions and rugs. I shall meet you at the garden gate—but it is understood," she added with a subtle smile, "I shan't intrude. You'll remember the address? There will be a brand-new streetlight in front of the gate."

"Oh, one thing," said Erwin, collecting his courage. "Let them be dressed at first—I mean let them look just as they were when I chose them—and let them be very merry and loving."

"Why, naturally," she replied, "everything will be just as you wish whether you tell me or not. Otherwise there was no point in starting the whole business, *n'est-ce pas?* Confess, though, my dear boy—you were on the brink of enrolling me in your harem. No, no, have no fear, I am kidding you. Well, that's your stop. Very wise to call it a day. Five is fine. See you a few secs after midnight, ha-ha."

4

Upon reaching his room, Erwin took off his shoes and stretched out on the bed. He woke up toward evening. A mellifluous tenor at full blast streamed from a neighbor's phonograph: *"I vant to be happee—"*

Erwin started thinking back: Number one, the Maiden in White, she's the most artless of the lot. I may have been a little hasty. Oh, well, no harm done. Then the Twins near the pillar of glass. Gay, painted young things. With them I'm sure to have fun. Then number four, Leilla the Rose, resembling a boy. That's, perhaps, the best one. And finally, the Fox in the ale-house. Not bad either. But only five. That's not very many!

He lay prone for a while with his hands behind his head, listening to the tenor, who kept wanting to be happy: Five. No, that's absurd. Pity it's not Monday morning: those three shopgirls the other day—oh, there are so many more beauties waiting to be found! And I can always throw in a streetwalker at the last moment.

Erwin put on his regular pair of shoes, brushed his hair, and hurried out.

By nine o'clock he had collected two more. One of them he noticed in a café where he had a sandwich and two drams of Dutch gin. She was talking with great animation to her companion, a beard-fingering foreigner, in an impenetrable language—Polish or Russian—and her gray eyes had a slight slant, her thin aquiline nose wrinkled when she laughed, and her elegant legs were exposed to the knee. While Erwin watched her quick gestures, the reckless way in which she tap-tapped cigarette ash all over the table, a German word, like a window, flashed open in her Slavic speech, and this chance word *("offenbar")* was the "evident" sign. The other girl, number seven on the list, turned up at the Chinese-style entrance of a small amusement park. She wore a scarlet blouse with a bright-green skirt, and her bare neck swelled as she shrieked in glee, fighting off a couple of slap-happy young boors who were grabbing her by the hips and trying to make her accompany them.

"I'm willing, I'm willing!" she cried out at last, and was rushed away.

Varicolored paper lanterns enlivened the place. A sledgelike affair with wailing passengers hurtled down a serpentine channel, disappeared in the angled arcades of medieval scenery, and dived into a new abyss with new howls. Inside a shed, on four bicycle seats (there were no wheels, just the frames, pedals, and handlebars), sat four girls in jerseys and shorts—a red one, a blue one, a green, a yellow one—their bare legs working at full tilt. Above them hung a dial on which moved four pointers, red, blue, green, and yellow. At first the blue one was first, then the green overtook it. A man with a whistle stood by and collected the coins of the few simpletons who wanted to place their bets. Erwin stared at those magnificent legs, naked nearly up to the groin and pedaling with passionate power.

They must be terrific dancers, he thought; I could use all four.

The pointers obediently gathered into one bunch and came to a stop.

"Dead heat!" shouted the man with the whistle. "A sensational finish!"

Erwin drank a glass of lemonade, consulted his watch, and made for the exit.

Eleven o'clock and eleven women. That will do, I suppose.

He narrowed his eyes as he imagined the pleasures awaiting him. He was glad he had remembered to put on clean underwear.

How slyly Frau Monde put it, reflected Erwin with a smile. Of course she will spy on me and why not? It will add some spice.

He walked, looking down, shaking his head delightedly, and only rarely glancing up to check the street names. Hoffmann Street, he knew was quite far, but he still had an hour, so there was no need to hurry. Again, as on the previous night, the sky swarmed with stars and the asphalt glistened like smooth water, absorbing and lengthening the magic lights of the town. He passed a large cinema whose radiance flooded the sidewalk, and at the next corner a short peal of childish laughter caused him to raise his eyes.

He saw before him a tall elderly man in evening clothes with a little girl walking beside—a child of fourteen or so in a low-cut black party dress. The whole city knew the elderly man from his portraits. He was a famous poet, a senile swan, living all alone in a distant suburb. He strode with a kind of ponderous grace; his hair, the hue of soiled cotton wool, reached over his ears from beneath his fedora. A stud in the triangle of his starched shirt caught the gleam of a lamp, and his long bony nose cast a wedge of shadow on one side of his thin-lipped mouth. In the same tremulous instant Erwin's glance lit on the face of the child mincing at the old poet's side; there was something odd about that face, odd was the flitting glance of her much too shiny eyes, and if she were not just a little girl—the old man's granddaughter, no doubt—one might suspect that her lips were touched up with rouge. She walked swinging her hips very, very slightly, her legs moved closer together, she was asking her companion something in a ringing voice—and although Erwin gave no command mentally, he knew that his swift secret wish had been fulfilled.

"Oh, of course, of course," replied the old man coaxingly, bending toward the child.

They passed, Erwin caught a whiff of perfume. He looked back, then went on.

"Hey, careful," he suddenly muttered as it dawned upon him that this made twelve—an even number: I must find one more—within half an hour.

It vexed him a little to go on searching, but at the same time he was pleased to be given yet another chance.

I'll pick up one on the way, he said to himself, allaying a trace of panic. I'm sure to find one!

"Maybe, it will be the nicest of all," he remarked aloud as he peered into the glossy night.

And a few minutes later he experienced the familiar delicious contraction—that chill in the solar plexus. A woman in front of him was walking along with rapid and light steps. He saw her only from the back and could not have explained why he yearned so poignantly to overtake precisely *her* and have a look at her face. One might, naturally, find random words to describe her bearing, the movement of her shoulders, the silhouette of her hat—but what is the use? Something beyond visible outlines, some kind of special atmosphere, an ethereal excitement, lured Erwin on and on. He marched fast and still could not catch up with her; the humid reflections of lights flickered before him; she tripped along steadily, and her black shadow would sweep up, as it entered a streetlamp's aura, glide across a wall, twist around its edge, and vanish.

"Goodness, I've got to see her face," Erwin muttered. "And time is flying."

Presently he forgot about time. That strange silent chase in the night intoxicated him. He managed at last to overtake her and went on, far ahead, but had not the courage to look back at her and merely slowed down, whereupon she passed him in her turn and so fast that he did not have time to raise his eyes. Again he was walking ten paces behind her and by then he knew, without seeing her face, that she was his main prize. Streets burst into colored light, petered out, glowed again; a square had to be crossed, a space of sleek blackness, and once more with a brief click of her high-heeled shoe the woman stepped onto a sidewalk, with Erwin behind, bewildered, disembodied, dizzy from the misty lights, the damp night, the chase.

What enticed him? Not her gait, not her shape, but something else, bewitching and overwhelming, as if a tense shimmer surrounded her: mere fantasy, maybe, the flutter, the rapture of fantasy, or maybe it was that which changes a man's entire life with one divine stroke—Erwin knew nothing, he just sped after her over asphalt and stone, which seemed also dematerialized in the iridescent night.

Then trees, vernal lindens, joined the hunt: they advanced whispering on either side, overhead, all around him; the little black hearts of their shadows intermingled at the foot of each streetlamp, and their delicate sticky aroma encouraged him.

Once again Erwin came near. One more step, and he would be abreast of her. She stopped abruptly at an iron wicket and fished out her keys from her handbag. Erwin's momentum almost made him bump into her. She turned her face toward him, and by the light a streetlamp cast through emerald leaves, he recognized the girl who had been playing that morning with a woolly black pup on a graveled path, and immediately remembered, immediately understood all her charm, tender warmth, priceless radiance.

He stood staring at her with a wretched smile.

"You ought to be ashamed of yourself," she said quietly. "Leave me alone."

The little gate opened, and slammed. Erwin remained standing under the hushed lindens. He looked around, not knowing which way to go. A few paces away, he saw two blazing bubbles: a car standing by the sidewalk. He went up to it and touched the motionless, dummylike chauffeur on the shoulder.

"Tell me what street is this? I'm lost."

"Hoffmann Street," said the dummy dryly.

And then a familiar, husky, soft voice spoke out of the depths of the car.

"Hello. It's me."

Erwin leaned a hand on the car door and limply responded.

"I am bored to death," said the voice, "I'm waiting here for my boyfriend. He is bringing the poison. He and I are dying at dawn. How are you?"

"Even number," said Erwin, running his finger along the dusty door.

"Yes, I know," calmly rejoined Frau Monde. "Number thirteen turned out to be number one. You bungled the job rather badly."

"A pity," said Erwin.

"A pity," she echoed, and yawned.

Erwin bowed, kissed her large black glove, stuffed with five outspread fingers, and with a little cough turned into the darkness. He walked with a heavy step, his legs ached, he was oppressed by the thought that tomorrow was Monday and it would be hard to get up.

excerpts from
tHe DeviL's DicTiONaRY

by AMBROSE BIERCE

a

ADMIRATION, *n.* Our polite recognition of another's resemblance to ourselves.

B

BORE, *n.* A person who talks when you wish him to listen.

C

CABBAGE, *n.* A familiar kitchen-garden vegetable about as large and wise as a man's head.

D

DELUGE, *n.* A notable first experiment in baptism which washed away the sin (and sinners) of the world.

e

EDIBLE, *adj.* Good to eat, and wholesome to digest, as a worm to a toad, a toad to a snake, a snake to a pig, a pig to a man, and a man to a worm.

f

FRIENDSHIP, *n.* A ship big enough to carry two in fair weather, but only one in foul.

g

GRAVE, *n.* A place in which the dead are laid to await the coming of the medical student.

H

HEARSE, *n.* Death's baby-carriage.

I

IMPIETY, *n.* Your irreverence toward my deity.

J

JEALOUS, *adj.* Unduly concerned about the preservation of that which can be lost only if not worth keeping.

k

KILL, *v.t.* To create a vacancy without nominating a successor.

L

LANGUAGE, *n.* The music with which we charm the serpents guarding another's treasure.

m

MARTYR, *n.* One who moves along the line of least reluctance to a desired death.

N

NOISE, *n.* A stench in the ear. Undomesticated music. The chief product and authenticating sign of civilization.

O

ONCE, *adv.* Enough.

P

PIRACY, *n.* Commerce without its folly-swaddles, just as God made it.

Q

QUILL, *n.* An implement of torture yielded by a goose and commonly wielded by an ass. This use of the quill is now obsolete, but its modern equivalent, the steel pen, is wielded by the same everlasting Presence.

R

REASON, *v.i.* To weigh probabilities in the scales of desire.

S

SAINT, *n.* A dead sinner revised and edited.

t

TELEPHONE, *n.* An invention of the devil which abrogates some of the advantages of making a disagreeable person keep his distance.

U

UN-AMERICAN, *adj.* Wicked, intolerable, heathenish.

V

VIRTUES, *n. pl.* Certain abstentions.

y

YEAR, *n.* A period of three hundred and sixty-five disappointments.

Z

ZEAL, *n.* A certain nervous disorder afflicting the young and inexperienced. A passion that goeth before a sprawl.

When Zeal sought Gratitude for his reward
He went away exclaiming: "O my Lord!"
"What do you want?" the Lord asked, bending down.
"An ointment for my cracked and bleeding crown."
Jum Coople

Therefore it behooveth hire a full long spoon
that shal eat with a feend.

CHAUCER

ou don't like me, I know, and that makes me sad. My help may nevertheless still come in handy. The devil is not as black as they like to paint him. True, you annoyed me yesterday, but I won't hold it against you today, and I have after all made the road seem shorter, this you must admit. Why don't you just try your shadow back on for size?"

The sun had risen, people were approaching us on the road; I accepted his proposition, albeit reluctantly. Grinning, he let my shadow unravel and fall to the ground, and it immediately took its place beside the horse's shadow, both of them trotting merrily along. How strange I felt. I rode past a party of country bumpkins, who doffed their hats and humbly made way for a man of means. I rode on, peering down with a greedy eye and a beating heart at the shadow, formerly mine, which I had just borrowed back from a stranger, indeed from my mortal enemy.

Bemused, indifferent to my chagrin, he strode beside me, absentmindedly whistling a little tune. He on foot, I on horseback, the giddiness of the idea went to my head, the temptation was too great, all of a sudden I seized the reins, dug in with my spurs, and made a mad dash for it; the shadow, however, refused to follow, but pivoted free of the horse and paused, awaiting the arrival of its rightful owner. Red-faced with shame, I was obliged to turn back, while the man in the gray coat calmly finished whistling his little ditty and, laughing at me, reattached the shadow and warned that it would stick to my feet and stay with me only when I could again lay claim to it as my rightful possession. "I've got you by your shadow," he continued, "no sense trying to escape. A rich man like you needs a respectable shadow, there's no getting around it; it's just too bad you didn't see reason long ago."

ADELBERT VON CHAMISSO
from *Peter Schlemiel*

excerpts from

the master and margarita

by MIKHAIL BULGAKOV

Just then the sultry air coagulated and wove itself into the shape of a man—a transparent man of the strangest appearance. On his small head was a jockey cap, and he wore a short check jacket fabricated of air. The man was seven feet tall but narrow in the shoulders, incredibly thin and with a face made for derision.

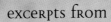

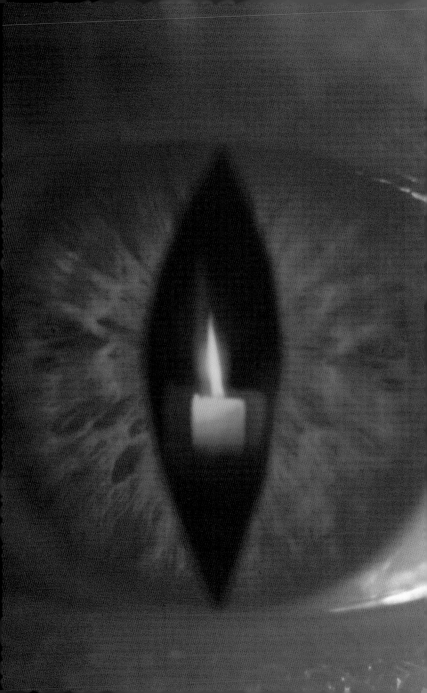

Two eyes bored into Margarita's face. In the depths of the right eye was a golden spark that could pierce any soul to its core; the left eye was as empty and black as a small black diamond, as the mouth of a bottomless well of darkness and shadow. Woland's face was tilted to one side, the right-hand corner of his mouth pulled downward, and deep furrows marked his forehead running parallel to his eyebrows. The skin of his face seemed burned by timeless sunshine.

Woland was lying sprawled on the bed, dressed only in a long, dirty, black nightshirt, patched on the left shoulder. . . .

On Woland's bare, hairless chest Margarita noticed a scarab on a gold chain, intricately carved out of black stone and engraved with an arcane script.

Afterward, when it was frankly too late, various persons collected their data and issued descriptions of this man. As to his teeth, he had platinum crowns on the left side and gold ones on the right. He wore an expensive gray suit and foreign shoes of the same color as his suit. His gray beret was stuck jauntily over one ear and under his arm he carried a walking stick with a knob in the shape of a poodle's head. He looked slightly over forty. Crooked sort of mouth. Clean-shaven. Dark hair. Right eye black, left eye for some reason green. Eyebrows black, but one higher than the other. In short—a foreigner.

The Devil is good when he is pleased.

JOHN CLARKE

Income tax has made liars of
more people than the devil.

WILL ROGERS

IF GOD DIDN'T EXIST, WOULD THE PIOUS BEHAVE SHAMELESSLY?

if the DEVIL DIDN'T exist, WOULD the CRUEL BE KINDER?

I am a professional persuader; our kind is legion. We are promoters and politicians, actors and hucksters, talk show hosts and televangelists, lounge lizards and Lotharios, the slippery and the saintly. We spend our days and nights manipulating minds, hoping, in turn, to produce changes in behavior. Have you ever played with a string puppet, or pushed a row of dominoes? The process is much the same, but because our toys possess free will and hold notions of their own, I liken it to a form of animal training.

Occasionally, we compete with one another. Perhaps you have seen me in some quaint painting, tugging at the

sleeve of some sinner on his deathbed, while loved ones, heavenly beings, or The Big One Himself hovers in anticipation. We extend discreet professional courtesies and avoid public displays. Influence, for us, is a gentleman's pastime, not a school-yard brawl, and whether you see our work as good or evil depends entirely on your perspective.

Methods of persuasion are our tools, and like many of my colleagues, I use the best. Some are well worn: use has molded their grips and deepened their patinas. The following pages reveal a few of the classic implements of our various trades. Perhaps you will find, as I have, that a tool's true beauty is in its skillful employ. I invite you to inspect and admire these selections from my collection.

the prying tools
empathy and sympathy

❧

Who doesn't respond to empathy? (Even I ask for sympathy.) But remember, subtle application is the trick. A delicate touch wins trust with ease, allowing you to breach those stubborn defenses. Act clumsily and you might as well move on to another victim.

If you want some poor fool's soul (or vote, money, or sexual favors), use empathy first. Acquaint yourself, from the inside out, with the weaknesses of your intended. Our culture teaches that the capacity to empathize is a virtue, which makes it easy to take full advantage of any crack in the psyche's armor. I, however, would classify it as a skill. Think of opening an oyster: locate the chinks, then loosen with empathy, pry with sympathy. A steady, rocking pressure opens the vulnerable passages easily and leaves them hard to close.

the devil's tools are sharp and sleek and if used well will never squeak.

the adjusting tools
the presumption of goodness, piety, and virtue

❧

How easy it is to claim virtue today! Even I am appalled. Despite their declarations, I recognize my sanctimonious colleagues for what they really are, and though I blush at their tactics, I admire their skills. They remind me that the most successful persuaders always claim moral superiority. It's the next handy tool.

Of course, media hucksters have a clear advantage here. Using solid professional training and a natural talent for deceit, they swiftly remove their victims from the influence of sense and logic. And if these manipulators can believe their own deceptions, how much more irresistible their powers of inducement!

flee if you can and plead if
you wish, but good luck ducking
the well-aimed pitch.

the reinforcing tools
a prize in every box

🍂

When you see your influence working, don't skimp on rewards. Pleasures once enjoyed are difficult to relinquish, so this is no time for false economies. Before proceeding, display every enticement you have to offer: riches, fame, comfort, love, or salvation (the big one). Your victim's dependence on these luxuries will allow you to sink your hook a little deeper.

if his trick you wish repeat'd, you must be sure the dog's well treat'd.

the DIVISIVE tooLs
fear, guiLt, bLame

❧

Fear is the all-in-one tool. How well it works to stig-matize, segregate, isolate, and paralyze! It's as effective on an entire population as on a lonely soul, and its range is awesome.

To most professional persuaders, fear is the ultimate utility, but you may be surprised to learn that it is not my tool of choice. Simply scaring the wits out of some-one is child's play for a gifted gentleman like myself. I prefer whittling away, one-on-one, using guilt and blame like the twin blades of a pocketknife. I find it vastly more entertaining to follow a victim who is wracked by remorse, jealousy, or vindictiveness, antici-pating the moment when the poor sot resorts to pitiful pleadings, ridiculous promises, and the delicious squan-dering of his dignity. To you, mine may not be the most agreeable of implements, but mark my words:

serve up fat portions of
fear, guiLt, and bLame
to render a tough man
sad, weak, and Lame.

the restraining tools
intolerance, hatred, exclusion, distrust

❦

Backsliders are trouble, but proper maintenance will keep most of your converts on the straight and narrow.

How do successful persuaders retain their flocks, their pets, their victims? Once again, fear is the best tool for this job. Not the scary, adrenaline jolt from a horror movie or sweaty nightmare. Nor the lurking shadow in the bushes that turns out to be nothing more than a shadow in the bushes. My first choice is a yeasty fear that can grow into something mean and irrational. This requires intolerance, hatred, exclusion, and distrust. Impulses as old as I am. Was I not, in fact, their very first victim?

place your bets on imaginary threats.

CONCLUSION, OR ILLUSION?

❧

James Agee wrote: "I am not sure but what Puritanism is the slickest disguise of the greatest of the earthly devils." He knew that those who profess to do "good" use the same tools and methods of influence as those who knowingly do "evil." He also knew that evil can grow out of a good impulse, and that good can grow from an evil one.

In the end, the consumer, the convert, the parishioner, the soldier, the lover, the patriot, the mark, and the slave are all, to varying degrees, manipulated beings. My advice to you, reader: heads up, eyes open. I am right behind you, just where God put us—me and my fellow persuaders.

Care to speculate on His motives?
That's another story.

the patterns of your behavior

reveal my methods

copyrights and credits

Every effort has been made to trace the ownership of copyrighted material. If errors or omissions have occurred, they will be corrected in subsequent editions upon notification in writing to the publisher.

text

Page 12   "Satan's Letter" from *Letters from the Earth* by Mark Twain, edited by Bernard DeVoto. Copyright 1938, 1944, 1946, 1959, 1962 by The Mark Twain Company. Copyright renewed. Reprinted by permission of HarperCollins Publishers, Inc.

Page 14   From *Pictures of Travels: The Return Home* by Heinrich Heine.

Page 16   From *Magic, Supernaturalism and Religion* by Kurt Seligmann, copyright © 1948 by Pantheon Books. Reprinted by permission of the publisher.

Page 29   From *Paradise Lost,* Book IV, by John Milton.

Page 31   From *Paradise Lost,* Book I, by John Milton.

Pages 32–33   Selected excerpts from *The Revolt of the Angels,* chs. 18 and 35, by Anatole France.

Page 40   Copyright © 1982 by Jenny Holzer. Used by permission of Jenny Holzer.

Page 64   From *The Devil: An Historical Critical and Medical Study,* ch. 5, by Maurice Garçon and Jean Vinchon. Copyright © 1930 by E. P. Dutton & Co.

Page 71   "Satan's Wiles" by Billy Graham. Reprinted by permission of Tribune Media Services.

Page 90   From *The Man Who Fell in Love with the Moon* by Tom Spanbauer. Copyright © 1991 by Atlantic Monthly Press.

Pages 103–7   Exerpts from "The Painter's Bargain" by William Thackeray.

Pages 121–35   "A Nursery Tale" from *The Stories of Vladimir Nabokov* by Vladimir Nabokov. Copyright © 1995 by Dmitri Nabokov. Reprinted by permission of Alfred A. Knopf Inc.

Page 143   From *Peter Schlemiel: The Man Who Sold His Shadow* by Adelbert Von Chamisso, translated by Peter Wortsman. Copyright © 1993 by Fromm International Publishing Corp. Reprinted by permission of Fromm International Publishing Corp.

Page 145–49   Selected excerpts from *The Master and Margarita* by Mikhail Bulgakov and translated by Michael Glenny. English language translation © 1967 by The Harvill Press, London and Harper & Row, New York. Copyright renewed 1995. Reprinted outside Britain and the British Commonwealth by permission of HarperCollins Publishers, Inc. First published in Great Britain by The Harvill Press 1967. © in the English translation by Michael Glenny, The Harvill Press and Harper & Row, Publishers, Inc. 1967. Reprinted in Britain and the British Commonwealth by permission of The Harvill Press.

iLLustrations

Photos by Ed Marquand except as follows:

Cover: Collection of Dolph Gotelli.

Pages 16 & 17   Andrea di Bonaiuto. *Christ Carrying the Cross, Crucifixion, and Descent into Limbo* (details). Spanish Chapel, Santa Maria Novella, Florence. Photo: Scala/Art Resource, New York

Page 18   Collection of Martha Avery.

Page 19   *Tahmuras Defeats the Divs* (detail). Iran. The Metropolitan Museum of Art, New York, Gift of Arthur A. Houghton, Jr., 1970 (1970.301.3). © 1996 by The Metropolitan Museum of Art.

Page 20   Heinrich Kley, sketch.

Pages 20–21   Marcel Duchamp, Untitled, from *Minotaure Magazine* #6 (winter 1935). Courtesy Richard Lorenz. © 1996 Artists Rights Society (ARS), New York / ADAGP, Paris. Photo: M. Lee Fatherree

Page 23   Marco Prozzo, *Into the Void*, 1996.

Page 24   *The Apocalypse of St. John*. France, 9th c. Bibliothèque Municipale, Cambrai, France. Photo: Giraudon

Page 25   Pol de Limbourg, *Fall of the Rebel Angels*, from *Les Très Riches Heures du Duc de Berry*, folio 64. France, ca. 15th c. Musée Condé, Chantilly, France. Photo: Giraudon

Page 26   *Saint Michael*. Mexico. San Antonio Museum of Art, San Antonio, Texas.

Pages 27, 28–29, 30, 32   Gustave Doré, engravings, 19th c. Photos: Rob Vinnedge

Pages 34 & 35   *Universal Judgment* (details), 12–13th c. Basilica, Torcello, Italy.

Pages 36–37   Domenico di Michelino, *Dante, Heaven and Hell*. Photo: David Lees/Corbis

Pages 38 & 39   Simon Marmion (attrib.), *Les Visions du Chevalier Tondal*, folios 13v and 17 (details). J. Paul Getty Museum, Los Angeles.

Page 41   Woodcut. Germany, 16th c.

Page 42   Master of Catherine of Cleves, *Mouth of Hell*, from *Book of Hours of Catherine of Cleves* (M.945), folio 168v (detail). Netherlands, ca. 1435. The Pierpont Morgan Library, New York. Photo: Art Resource

Page 43   Master of Catherine of Cleves, *Release of Souls from the Mouth of Hell*, from *Book of Hours of Catherine of Cleves* (M.945), folio 107 (detail). Netherlands, ca. 1440. The Pierpont Morgan Library, New York. Photo: Art Resource

Pages 44–45   Gustave Doré, *Lucifer, King of Hell*. Engraving from Dante's *Divine Comedy*, 1868. Photo: Rob Vinnedge

Page 46   Hugo van der Goes, *The Fall of Man*, 15th c. Kunsthistorisches Museum, Vienna.

Pages 48–49   Michelangelo, *The Fall of Man*, 1508–12. Sistine Chapel, Vatican Palace, Vatican City. Photo: A. Bracchetti–P. Zigrossi, Vatican Museums

Page 50   Duane Michals, *The Fallen Angel*, nos. 1 and 8, 1968. Used by permission of the artist.

Page 52   Jan Mandyn Van Haarlem, *The Last Judgement*. Museum of Fine Arts, Springfield, Mass., James Philip Gray Collection.

Pages 54–55   Marco Prozzo, *The Ladder of Life*, 1996.

Page 56   Jean Colombe, *Hell*, from *Les Très Riches Heures du Duc de Berry*, folio 108v. France,

15th c. Musée Condé, Chantilly, France. Photo: Giraudon

Pages 58–59   *Christ in Limbo*. Museum of Fine Arts, Springfield, Mass., James Philip Gray Collection.

Pages 60 & 61   *The Roads to Hell and to Heaven*, United States, ca. 1830. Collection of Sam and Elizabeth Davidson. Photo: William Wickett

Pages 62–63   J. G. Posada, woodcut, late 19th–early 20th c.

Page 64   Collection of Ed Marquand.

Page 65   Photo: Marsha Burns

Pages 66–67   Duccio, *The Temptation of Christ on the Mountain* (detail). Copyright © The Frick Collection, New York.

Page 69   Gustave Doré, *Then was Jesus led up of the spirit into wilderness to be tempted of the devil*, 19th c. Photo: Rob Vinnedge

Page 70   Juan de Flandes, *The Temptation of Christ*, ca. 1500. Ailsa Mellon Bruce Fund, Copyright © 1996 Board of Trustees, National Gallery of Art, Washington, D.C.

Page 74   Michael Pacher, *The Devil Shows St. Augustine the Book of Blasphemy*, 1435–98. Alte Pinakothek, Munich. Photo: Artothek

Page 75 (top)   *St. Antoine lacéré par les Demons*. Photo: Francis G. Mayer/Corbis

Page 75 (bottom)   Collection of Ed Marquand.

Page 76   Max Ernst, *The Blessed Virgin Chastising the Infant Jesus before Three Witnesses: André Breton, Paul Eluard and the Painter*, 1926. Wallraf-Richartz Museum, Cologne. © 1996 Artists Rights Society (ARS), New York / SPADEM / ADAGP, Paris. Photo: Artothek

Page 77   Giovanni Pagani da Monterubbiano, *The Madonna of Mercy*, 1506. Musée du Petit Palais, Avignon, France.

Page 78   William Blake, *And Smote Job with Sore Boils* (top), and *Satan Himself Is Transformed into an Angel of Light* (bottom), from *Illustrations of the Book of Job*, ca. 1820, plates VI and XI. Collection of Sam and Elizabeth Davidson. Photos: William Wickett

Page 79   William Blake, *Satan, Sin and Death: Satan Comes to the Gates of Hell*, late 18th–early 19th c. The Henry E. Huntington Library and Art Gallery, San Marino, California.

Page 84 Jean-Jacques Feuchere, *Satan*, mid-19th c. Los Angeles County Museum of Art, Times Mirror Foundation, Los Angeles.

Page 90 Collection of Ed Marquand.

Page 100 Grotesque, Lincoln Cathedral, Lincolnshire, England, 12th c. Photo: Frederick Evans, 1891, courtesy Richard Lorenz

Page 104 *"Gossip" and Satan Came Also*. Collection of Ed Marquand.

Page 105 Wooden sculpture. Mexico. Collection of Dolph Gotelli. Photo: Ed Marquand

Page 106 Photo: John Hubbard

Page 112 Photo: Marco Prozzo

Page 113 Collection of Dolph Gotelli. Photo: Ed Marquand

Pages 114–15 Photo: Marsha Burns

Page 119 Grotesque, Lincoln Cathedral, Lincolnshire, England, 12th c. Photo: Frederick Evans, 1891, courtesy Richard Lorenz

Page 121 Rebecca Faeth Bird, *Untitled*, 1995. Collection of Susan E. Kelly.

Page 136 British broadside (detail), 19th c. Collection of Ed Marquand.

Pages 140–41 Ceramic figure. Mexico. Collection of Dolph Gotelli. Photo: Ed Marquand

Pages 144–45 Photo: Marsha Burns

Pages 148–49 Photo: Marsha Burns

Page 150 Sister Juana Beatriz de la Fuente, *La Pastorela (The Tree of Life)*. Mexico, 1805. San Antonio Museum of Art, San Antonio, Texas.

Page 151 Collection of Ed Marquand.

Pages 154 & 155 top Circus posters. Collection of Ed Marquand. Photos: Rob Vinnedge

Pages 156 & 157 Masks. Collection of Dolph Gotelli. Photos: Ed Marquand

Pages 158–59 Jerald Frampton, *Boy and Mask*, 1989. Copyright © Jerald Frampton.

Page 160 Chan Ku Yi, *The Senator Vanquishes the Devil*, 1996. Collection of Ed Marquand. Photo: Rob Vinnedge

Page 161 Chan Ku Yi, *The Devil Vanquishes the Senator*, 1996. Collection of Ed Marquand. Photo: Rob Vinnedge

Pages 162–63 Marco Prozzo, *The Devil's Toolbox*, 1996.

Page 165 *Heaven or Heck, A Sinner's Struggle*. Mexico. Collection of Deb Colburn.

Dedicated to my buddies Ralph,
the Pats, Jesse, Phyllis, and Bob.
So bad and so clever.

❧

Literary condensations by Laura Iwasaki
Edited by Laura Iwasaki and Marie Weiler with Nancy Grubb
Designed by Ed Marquand and John Hubbard with assistance by Randalee Maddox
Produced by Marquand Books, Inc., Seattle
Printed and bound by Midas Printing Limited, Hong Kong

Library of Congress Cataloging-in-Publication Data
The devil's mischief : in which his own story is told in word and pictures / [edited by]
    Edward Bruce Marquand.
        p.   cm.
    ISBN 0-7892-0136-4
    1. Devil—Literary collections. 2. Devil in art. I. Marquand, Ed.
PN6071.D47D48   1996
809'.93351—dc20   96-12045

10 9 8 7 6 5 4 3 2 1

Many fine friends and colleagues have directed me to the art and literature used in this book. They include Andrea Augé, Lois Barry, Marsha Burns, Sam Davidson, Gail Gibson, Dolph Gotelli, Nancy Grubb, Laura Iwasaki, Susan Kelly, Richard Lorenz, Tom Matthiesen, Marion Oettinger, Marco Prozzo, Kerry Quint, Kiff Slemmons, Gillian Speeth, Claudia Vernia, and Pamela Zytnicki. Part of the pleasure in preparing an anthology lies in the conversations the activity sparks. Some of the most fruitful have been inspired by Colin Campbell, Michael Longyear, and John Stevenson. Preparation of this book has depended on the hard work, boundless talents, indulgence, and good humor of staff members at Marquand Books, including Jesi Asagi, Christina Gimlin, Manine Golden, John Hubbard, Carole Jordan, Susan Kelly, Tomarra LeRoy, Randalee Maddox, Craig Orbach, Keira Roberts, Noreen Ryan, Marta Vinnedge, Marie Weiler, and Pamela Zytnicki. Owen Dugan, Patricia Fabricant, Mark Magowan, and Myrna Smoot provided important support and suggestions all along.

    I am also indebted to two fine books: Robert Hughes's excellent work, *The History of Heaven and Hell in Western Art*, and Alice Turner's survey, *The History of Hell*.